KAREN CARLUCCI WAHNER

A Guide to Healing
Your Sassy Self

For Kristen, Katie, Justin, and Kimmy

-You were always my Why

Acknowledgments

This book could not have been written without the help of others and the life events I've experienced. Every good thing, as well as bad, has made me the person I am today, and I am grateful for what I have learned along the way. I wish to thank my kids, Kristen, Katie, Justin, and Kimmy for being incredibly beautiful people, and allowing me to bounce ideas off of them no matter how strange they sound. I also wish to thank Bruce, for giving me four of the most beautiful gifts I could have ever received in this lifetime and for suggesting that I write in order to maintain my sanity as a stay-at-home mom. I am grateful for my teacher, Mr. Daniel Loose, whose passion for the written word, and the ability to pull more details out of me, helped me to discover that I really loved to write. A big thank you goes out to my editors, Adrienne Dillard, Elizabeth Bell, along with Kristen and Katie, who took the time to make sure I didn't ramble on and totally destroy the English language. I truly appreciate all their help in this process. If you find any mistakes in the book, it's most likely my fault, not theirs, because I kept rewriting things that they already said were fine. Adrienne, my twin flame, I am incredibly grateful for all your support in every area of my life. I am so blessed to have you as a friend and as my touchstone. Thanks for talking me off the ledge more times than I care to count. Tammy, you haven't been in my life very long, but oh man, I love your moxie—thanks for caring. Special thanks to Jeff for your support. Finally, I wish to thank Spirit for guiding me to where I need to be. You have given me such incredible abundance in this life, and I am eternally grateful.

Table of Contents

Table of Contents

They tried to bury us,
They didn't know we were seeds

-Mexican Proverb

Introduction

I want to welcome you as you embark upon a new journey, my friend. I will be your guide along the way and my goal is to help you find the answers you seek. Not everything in this book will apply to everyone, but I believe that there is a great deal of information and guidance that will apply to all. You see, everyone has their own journey—no two are alike. Some of you have already traveled a long way while others are just starting out. For some of you, the roads have been relatively smooth with an occasional bump or two along the way while others have traveled through incredibly rough terrain. Our journeys should be filled with love, laughter, and joy, but are many times filled with stress, regret, and sadness. If you are tired of living a life that doesn't seem to have a purpose, or you feel as though you've lost yourself somewhere along the way, then this book is here to help you. It will help you better understand yourself so that you can start making some significant changes and finally live the life that you deserve.

I want to make something incredibly clear before you even begin reading this book. Your intelligence has nothing to do with the situations you are, or were, in. It has nothing to do with the mistakes or decisions you've made. Stop telling yourself that you are too smart to be where you are in life. Many smart people have been in the same situations, made the same mistakes or decisions, and have done the same things as you. You are not stupid. You are human. I know this because I was there, beating myself up and questioning my intelligence because of a choice I made or a situation I ended up in. I used to get so angry with myself. *How could I have allowed this*, whatever it was, *to happen? I'm too smart for this*. So, here's what I've discovered, my friend. You can be a genius, but if you don't feel good about yourself, weren't raised to be bold and unstoppable, or you've spent your life settling for less than you deserve, you'll end up in situations that aren't so good for you. Stop equating this with intelligence—you are incredibly smart and here's how I know this—you're reading a book to get help to figure it out. You're seeking out resources to assist you with fulfilling your dream of a better life. As you read through this book, you'll begin to understand why you've gotten into certain situations or made certain decisions in your life, and once you understand the problem, you'll be able to figure out the solution.

The idea behind this book is to take you on a journey, and each chapter builds upon the previous one. My advice is to start at the beginning of the book and work your way to the end. This will provide you with a better understanding of moxie, where it went, and how best to reclaim it. I also suggest you grab a journal and keep it nearby because there are some exercises and writing prompts throughout the book that you'll want to use to help you in the healing process. In addition to the exercises and prompts, feel free to write down any other thoughts or ideas that come to mind as you are reading. I find that I can be most creative when I'm in self-discovery mode.

Remember, it only takes one creative idea to change your life, so keep that journal handy and allow the thoughts to flow. Since everyone is on their own individual journey, this book will be what it needs to be for each person. You may read some chapters and not see yourself in them, or you may have many *aha* moments in another. There are some chapters that you may get through very quickly while others may take some time. This is not a race, so go at the pace that you're most comfortable with.

I wrote this book as if I were talking to a friend, so don't be put off by the conversational tone of my writing. The contractions, slang, and sometimes colorful words I chose are intentional. If, for some reason, you're agitated by all the contractions, slang, and colorful words, then it might be a good idea for you to read this book, because if you're worried about that stuff instead of the content, then you probably need a good kick in the ass to remind you about what's really important in life. My suggestion to you is to keep reading. For the rest of you, who need a good friend at this time, pull up a chair, grab a glass of wine, or pour another cup of coffee—I've got some stuff I want to share with you.

Union Joe Stirs Some Moxie

*M*any years ago, when I was in my twenties, I had a friend named Lil who was in her forties. The age difference should have meant something, but it didn't—we were two peas in a pod. A woman with a petite frame and muted blonde hair, Lil was originally from Scotland and came over to the United States when she was in her twenties. Although she had been here for many years, she still had that Scottish brogue that I loved listening to and sometimes made fun of. Lil was a lot of fun and we spent a good portion of our time together laughing, drinking coffee, going out to dinner, and shopping. I remember stopping by her house one Saturday evening, just to hang out, as I often did.

Lil's husband, Joe, was home that night, sitting on the sofa watching television as he often spent his Saturday nights. Joe looked like someone who had been in the boxing ring or a bar fight quite a few times throughout his life. He was tough as nails and could often be found sitting on the sofa in his wife-beater t-shirt, his brown hair slicked back and a grimace on his face as he puffed away on his cigarettes. He had what reminded me of a boxer's nose, because it was crooked and slightly disjointed. I often wondered how his nose ended up looking like that, but never had the opportunity to bring it up in any of our conversations. I must admit there was a part of me that was somewhat afraid to ask. Joe was a no-nonsense guy and looked like he could pretty much handle anything you sent his way. Total tough guy who didn't take shit from anyone.

So, there I was, just sitting myself down in a chair across the sofa from Joe, and Lil was sitting on the chair off to the side in between us. Lil and I were having our usual small talk conversation about nothing in particular when she happened to ask what I did that day. I mentioned that I had done some food shopping at our local Mega Fresh grocery store, and I was starting to list off the deals I had gotten, when I heard Joe's voice reaching a volume slightly over mine.

"Fucking scabs." It wasn't a yell, it was just merely a grumbling statement.

I furrowed my brow, cocked my head to the left and looked over at him. I can only imagine the perplexed look on my face as I said, "Excuse me?"

"The people at Mega Fresh are union-busting scabs. That company doesn't pay a union wage. They're nothing but fucking scabs," he says and then takes a drag on his cigarette.

Now is a good time to tell you that Joe was a union guy all the way. He lived and breathed union, and I pitied the guy who tried to cross the union picket line if Joe was walking it. But unions didn't mean anything to me. I was never in one, and other than Joe, I didn't really know anyone who worked in a union. Joe worked for another local grocery store which was obviously union. So not only was I shopping at the competitor, but I was shopping at the nonunion competitor.

Look, I was just trying to save a buck or two, not get into a debate that night. I looked over at Lil and noticed a somewhat worried look on her face, as if she knew this conversation was not going to go so well. I looked back over at Joe, gave a little shrug and said, "Yeah, they may be nonunion, but I like shopping there. They've got some really great deals."

"They're cheaper because they don't pay union wages," he says.

"But that's really not my problem, Joe, I'm going to go wherever I can to save some money."

This is where he starts getting a wee bit louder.

"These places exist because people like you support scab companies. It makes it tougher for us union guys to get work and a decent wage."

I shoot a quick glance over at Lil in the hope of getting some support, but she's sitting in the chair with her eyes cast downward to avoid making eye contact with either of us. Her lips appear to be sealed tight. Apparently, she was not going to get involved in this one. I look back over at Joe.

"I like Mega Fresh," I firmly say back to him.

He takes another drag on his cigarette and is now sitting on the edge of the sofa. His face is red. I see some veins pulsing in his neck and his temples, and I can almost see the steam coming out of his ears.

With his eyes slightly squinted, he points his finger and cigarette at me.

"Now you listen to me," he says in a scary, gruff voice. "This is a union house. It's always been a union house. It's paid for thanks to the union. Our food is put on the table with union wages. We don't like scabs, and we don't appreciate those who do. Seems to me like you got a choice to make."

Really? I looked over at Lil, whose eyes were now opened so wide and bulging that I thought they might fall out of her head and roll across the floor. She looked back at me with that *I don't even know what to say or how to help you* expression on her face.

I looked back at Joe, squinted my eyes right back at him, leaned over, and said in a steady voice, "I like Mega Fresh. I'm shopping at Mega Fresh. My friends respect my choices. Seems to me like *you* got a choice to make."

A hush fell across the room. It was one of those uncomfortable and awkwardly long pauses. The air was thick and still, and Joe and I simply stared at one another. I could see Lil out of the corner of my eye. Her eyes were continuously shifting back and forth between Joe and me, I guess wondering how this standoff would eventually end.

Joe took another really long drag of his cigarette. The tip of it lighting up red to match the color of his face. The smoke filled his lungs for what seemed like an eternity. Then the exhale of smoke, which came right out through a narrow slit in his almost closed lips. He slowly leaned over towards me, his eyes which were just slits by this point, never leaving mine. Once again, the finger and cigarette were pointed my way.

Finally, he opened his mouth to speak. I thought, *Oh boy, here it comes.*

In the quietest of voices, almost a whisper, he leans in even closer towards me and says, "I like you kid. You got moxie."

With that, Joe snuffed out his cigarette in the ashtray, sat back in his sofa, and started watching television once again as if nothing had ever happened. I could feel an immediate change in the energy of the room. I looked over at Lil, whose shoulders were back to a relaxed state and her eyes appeared to be in a more natural position in their sockets. She seemed relieved that I didn't get thrown out of the house and we could head into the kitchen for our planned night of coffee and lively conversation.

Moxie. Joe said I had moxie.

I had no idea what moxie was or what it did, but it got the respect of Joe, so I knew it had to be something pretty damn special.

Is there Moxie in the House?

*A*fter my encounter with Union Joe, I went home that night and looked up the word moxie in the dictionary. I was curious to know what I could possibly have that made Joe want to take a step backward, and thereby, move me several steps up his respect ladder. The dictionary defined moxie as "a force of character, determination, or nerve." Wow, I thought, that was some powerful stuff considering it was such a funny little word. But, was that it? Was there anything else to this moxie thing? Surely there had to be more, so I decided to pull out my trusty pocket thesaurus. Yes, I really did have a pocket thesaurus back then, and I leafed through the pages until I found some synonyms in the thesaurus that were listed under the word moxie. What I found were some words that made me take a step back because of their strength. I encourage you to spend a moment or two reading those words out loud. Roll them off your tongue and see how good it feels. And as you're saying them, really feel the strength of the words.

Boldness.

Determination.

Fearlessness.

Fortitude.

Grit.

Guts.

Spunk.

Stamina.

Tenacity.

I have to admit that I especially like that last one, tenacity. There is nothing meek about any of those words. Just saying them out loud kind of makes you feel pretty gutsy, doesn't it? You might even find yourself standing up a little straighter or sticking that chin out just a touch bit more than usual just after you say them. It's as if you want to scream, "Hey world, I'm a total badass, and if you don't believe me, here's a few words to prove it."

Ever since that encounter with Union Joe, I have just fallen in love with the word moxie, or maybe it's just the visual of what gets conjured up when I think of it. You know, someone who speaks their mind with an immense air of confidence and doesn't allow their voice to be silenced. Either way, moxie is something we all need to have because it elevates us to our highest standards, without limits. It gives us power and strength. It also lets the rest of the world know that we're not taking shit from anyone.

But let's be clear, moxie is not strictly about toughness. Moxie is more about being true to yourself. It's about living a life of joy and happiness on your own terms, and it doesn't matter what those terms might be, because you are the only one who defines them. You are the only one who must be okay with them—no one else. It's about walking around with an air of confidence and a feeling of empowerment. It's speaking your voice and not worrying about what others think. It's about you marching to the beat of your own drum and not giving a rat's ass about what people have to say. When you have moxie, you get to be your authentic self. You become unstoppable. When you have moxie, you truly begin to understand your purpose in this life, and you gain a sense of urgency in fulfilling that purpose. The pieces fall into place and you hightail it to your intended destination. So how will you know when you've fully reclaimed your moxie? When you can stand alone, emit a light so bright and pure that no one can miss it, tell the world that you love yourself without judgement, and feel the power of universal love flowing through you to be shared with the world, then you my friend, have reclaimed your moxie.

I believe each of us is born with a great deal of moxie. When we are born, our moxie comes in the form of an incredibly bright light that beams from within, and spreads outward to the rest of the world. A light so bold and beautiful that it has the power to outshine all the ugliness of this world. It shines because we know nothing else, we only know love and innocence, and we have not yet encountered anything, or anyone, to stop it from shining.

From the moment of birth, we come onto this planet, filled to the brim with moxie, kicking and screaming for all to hear. It's as if we're saying to the world, "Yep, I'm here. Move over and get ready for some greatness!" And we are great—each and every one of us is a spectacular force to be reckoned with. We have so much greatness to offer this world and the beings that inhabit it. We come here with the purpose of making a difference in the lives of others and sharing our gifts with the entire world. In order to perform such an extraordinary task, we cannot let anything get in our way, so our moxie must thrive if we are to fulfill our purpose.

As infants, our moxie remains strong and comes through loud and clear. We think nothing of letting people know when we want or need something from someone. We have no problem making ourselves heard. Babies speak their voice often through crying and that voice is enough to get people to figure out the problem and quickly fix it.

"Hey you over there, I'm hungry. How about you put down what you're doing and get me something to eat."

"Whoa, whatever's going on in my diaper, I'm not liking it. Could you get over here and get this thing changed?"

As we transform from infants to toddlers, we manage to keep that moxie going. We start crawling to get where we need to go. We pull ourselves up using all our strength and whatever solid piece of furniture we can get our hands on. We show incredible determination to fulfill our goal. Then we take that bold first step, fall down, and get right back up to take some more. It doesn't matter how many times we fall, we keep getting right back up and taking another step. We don't quit until we've got it mastered. Now that's tenacity in action. But we don't stop there. Then we build upon our walking skills, and the next thing you know, we are running as fast and as hard as we can. Nothing holds us back at that age. We know no limits. We are unstoppable.

As we develop into young children, we continue to embrace that moxie we were born with. We begin to create. We finger-paint, build crazy shit with Legos, and draw lots of goofy looking stick-figure people. We are satisfied with our accomplishments and proudly show them off to whomever happens to cross our path. We don't second guess our talents as we create projects, and then wonder if they're good enough to show people. We put all our effort into them, do them once, and we're finished. We sing out loud and dance with enthusiasm, not knowing the correct words or steps, and not caring what the people watching us say or think. We explore the world around us with incredible wonder and we are not afraid, nor do we feel stupid, to ask questions. Lots of questions. We have a thirst for knowledge, and we will not relent until that thirst is quenched. We jump in puddles and don't care about getting wet. It's okay to get messy because it's fun. We love to have fun. Oh, and we laugh. We laugh with such pure enjoyment. We laugh so hard that we make others around us laugh too. People love to be in our presence because it makes them feel good.

As children, we live in our own beautiful world of love, innocence, and joy. Our moxie shines with an incredible brightness that lets the world know how truly awesome we are.

But then something happens.

Oh Where, Oh Where has my Moxie Gone?

While we are children, simple and silly rules start to become part of our lives. They begin to shape our mindset. We accept those rules because we trust what people tell us as being the truth. It's really not our fault. We don't know any better, so we begin to internalize those rules and accept them as our own.

"You can't jump in puddles, you'll get wet."

"Children should be seen and not heard."

"Boys don't play with dolls or wear pink."

"Girls don't play with trucks and are bad at math."

If we question those rules, we're immediately shut down, so we learn that it's better not to question things. We're reminded that this is the way things are, so don't rock the boat. Don't make waves. Just do as you're told. Unfortunately, this isn't good for us. Our beautiful moxie begins to dim. As we begin to grow older, and because of certain things that happen to us along the way, that magnificent, glowing light at the core of our being begins to dull a little bit more. We continue listening to people and their limiting beliefs. We take on their baggage. We even start to accept these limiting beliefs as our own.

"You'll never amount to much."

"You're going to end up just like your mother or father."

"Money is hard to come by."

"You can't make a living, let alone a career as an artist."

"You need a steady job with good benefits."

"You're never going to meet someone as nice as him or her."

Just imagine a candle burning brightly. Picture that flame as it flickers and grows with the oxygen that feeds it. Now imagine a candle snuffer sitting over top of that flame and slowing being lowered down. Imagine that beautiful flame being deprived of the oxygen necessary for it to burn. As the snuffer is lowered closer and closer to the flame, and finally makes contact with it, the flame is eventually snuffed out.

That, my friend, is what happens to our moxie.

Throughout our lives we meet people, or go through events, that essentially beat the hell out of our moxie. Sometimes we grow up in households that are not very nurturing. We may have had parents who were not very supportive of us or what we wanted to do in life.

I can remember loving music as a child. I grew up playing the violin and guitar for hours each day. I was in the school choir and orchestra. I even wrote my own music. I wanted to go to the high school for performing arts in my city, and focus on a career in music, but my mother made it quite clear that this was the most ridiculous idea ever and not even worthy of discussion. She also let me know that there was no future in being a musician. She had a way of cutting through me to make me feel really bad about any ideas I had. She could be quick to criticize. My father, in an effort to be supportive and always the peacemaker, told me to wait a bit and see how it goes, but by then the flame had already been greatly diminished. I did not go to the high school for performing arts. In fact, I would not pick up an instrument, or even sing again, for many years.

If you are a parent, I'm going to ask you to strongly consider the words that you speak to your children. Choose them carefully. Are they uplifting or are they critical? Do they empower and inspire, or do they discourage? People can easily take on the negative behaviors of their own parents without even recognizing it. Unless you make a conscious decision to change what has been done to you, you are destined to repeat it. Critical parenting begets critical parenting only when you allow it to. You alone have the power to change it.

Even before I had children, I made a commitment to myself that I would not discourage my children from being creative and following their own path in life. It was important that their flame burn as bright as possible. In fact, I used to tell them that there are enough people outside our door looking to tear us down, we will not do it to each other. Growing up in a household where I was repeatedly told "self-praise stinks" every time I was excited, and bragged about something I did, I fully understood how words affected children. If that's how you grew up, then I ask you to stop the cycle so that your kids grow up with their moxie intact.

Sometimes we lose our moxie because of other things that happen to us such as bad relationships, divorce, the loss of a job or a loved one. Traumatic events, or even significant disappointments we've had over the years, can also kick our moxie's ass. These events or experiences throw us for a loop and sometimes we find it difficult to recover energetically. Something as simple as hanging around people who do not share the same vibrational frequencies or values as us can cause a decrease in our moxie. I will talk more about energy and vibrational frequencies later, but for right now, understand that if your values or moral compass are higher than the people you are closest to, there is a good chance that your moxie will be diminished to match theirs.

Nothing beats the hell out of our moxie like an unhealthy intimate relationship. This type of relationship can wreak havoc in every area of your life, and that poor beaten down moxie will have a tough time coming back up to the full-tank level as long as you stay in that unhealthy relationship. Intimate relationships encompass our entire being, whether we like it or not. They touch on every aspect of our lives, and the energy of the relationship can raise your own energy to an "over-the-moon" feeling of empowerment and ecstasy, or draw you down to horrible depths of confusion, sadness, and desolation. Relationships are meant to be supportive, comforting, and filled with love and trust, but if you happen to be in one with someone who does not, or cannot, fulfill these basic requirements, then get ready for some moxie stomping.

There is no greater detriment to your moxie than being in a relationship with someone who lies to you (oh, and yes, this includes lies of omission), shows no generosity towards you (and I'm not necessarily talking about money), and essentially just makes you feel like shit every time you are around them. This is a toxic relationship. It is an energy vampire that will continue to suck out every last iota of your soul if you allow it to. Moxie cannot continue to thrive in a relationship that is not good for you. If your values and the values of your intimate partner are inherently different, then you've got a problem. Yes, we've all heard the term "opposites attract," and that may bide well with interests like cooking and sports, but it just won't jive with values and a moral compass. A horrible intimate relationship can continue to beat down on your moxie until there's almost nothing left of it. It can leave years of lasting damage to you and your psyche in the form of physical, emotional, and spiritual scars. If you are in a relationship that is not good for you, it might be best to think about what the future holds for you and where you really want to be in life. My best friend, Adrienne, once gave me some incredibly useful advice, and I'm going to pass it along to anyone who needs to read it. She said, "Stop looking for this to be the relationship you wanted, because clearly it's not. I know it's hard because you really want it to be that way, but it's not. The sooner you understand and accept that, the better off you will be." Those were some wise words, girlfriend!

Some of us have had a pattern throughout our lives of choosing the wrong people for relationships. Some of us have had to have the wind knocked out of our moxie quite a few times before getting the hint of who is, or isn't, in our best interest. If you are one of these people, and I'll admit I've been one, then it's time for you to understand that you really need to take a hard look at things. You must figure out why you're repeating this pattern and decide what you want for your life as far as intimate relationships go. It's time to stop settling for less than you deserve.

I want you to stop right here for a moment. If you have a journal or piece of paper, now would be a good time to grab it. I want you to picture the perfect person for you and start writing down their description. Who are they? What do they look like? What kind of things would they do for you? How would they make you feel? How would they treat you? What kind of life do you see with them? What would you be doing together? You can answer each question as a list or you can write a thesis, but really think about it and be specific. By doing this, you're essentially putting in your order with the universe for the perfect mate for you. And before you go all cynical about nobody being perfect, I'm not saying they are a perfect person, I'm simply saying they are a perfect mate. Big difference.

If you want the perfect mate, then you need to set the intention of attracting the perfect mate. Let's think about this. Most of the time we tend to take whoever happens to come our way without even thinking about it. We don't take the time to envision how we want our spouse or significant other to be. We meet them, fall in love, fall out of love because they're not what we wanted, and then start all over again. We take more time and effort to envision our next vacation, cell phone, or car than we do our significant other. If we *want* our relationships to be a certain way, then we must truly set the intention that they *will be* a certain way. As a real estate agent, I wouldn't simply run buyers around to a bunch of houses on a whim. They gave me specific details about the type of house they wanted to call home. Four bedrooms, two and a half baths, and a two-car garage sitting on an acre of ground. The house should also have a family room with a fireplace, a large modern eat-in kitchen, and a finished basement. That was the description they gave me and that is what I sought to give them. The universe is no different. Get specific with your request for your partner or relationship, set the intention, and trust that it will happen.

If you no longer happen to be in an unhealthy relationship, or never were in one, give yourself a big high-five and a well-deserved round of applause. You've earned it and you're well on your way to reclaiming your moxie. Obviously, there's some other stuff floating around in your past or present world, or you wouldn't be reading this book. Don't worry—there's plenty of moxie stompers to discover ahead— we'll get it figured out.

So far, we've only covered the intimate relationship moxie killers. There are other relationships you might be engaged in that could be doing some big-time moxie damage. These relationships could be with anyone such as friends, acquaintances, family members, coworkers, neighbors, or anyone else who could be putting a hurting on your precious moxie. Gossip, jealousy, belittling and tearing your self-image to shreds may be part of these relationships. Once again, I warn against being involved in toxic and abusive relationships. If a relationship does not seem to offer you any benefit, then you need to question why you are in it. Never feel obligated or guilted into keeping a relationship going just because you don't want to hurt someone's feelings. Know that you only deserve to be in relationships with people who are good for you and want to see you at your best. Don't allow the fear of being alone dictate the type of relationships you have. It's better to be in only a few relationships that are great for you than many which aren't.

I know we've talked a lot about losing our moxie due to unhealthy relationships, but there are other things that cause that moxie to dim. Sometimes moxie gets lost when we lose ourselves. When we lose sight of the people we used to be, who we are, or even who we are meant to be, we have a difficult time connecting with our moxie. We say things like, "I don't even recognize myself anymore" or "I feel like a shell of the person I once was." I can definitely relate to this.

At the end of 2001 I decided to stay home to raise my kids. I already had three children and was pregnant with my fourth. At that time, I seemed to have it all. I had spent a lengthy career as a pharmaceutical scientist and was just coming off eight years as an elected official in the town where I lived. I was an incredibly busy person, always running around getting things accomplished. But when I decided to stay home with the kids, I found that I had to give some things up—things like mental stimulation, talking to adults, and running my own schedule. Being home with the kids as a full-time mom totally turned my world upside down.

Now don't get me wrong, I love my kids, and it was my choice to stay at home with them. I felt it was an important job and I wanted to be the one who was raising them instead of a total stranger. I found that some women define their lives as moms. I did not. I always defined myself as someone with a career. I was simply a career woman who happened to be taking some time off to raise her kids. Although I wouldn't have traded that experience for the world and believed that my kids were better off because of my choice, I went from being someone in charge of her own life to someone who suddenly was living her life for everyone else. I slowly began to lose my identity and became unclear as to who I really was. I felt overwhelmed and underappreciated in this new role. I felt alone and isolated. It might have been somewhat different today since social media is at our disposal. This makes it easier to connect with others who are like us, but this was way before social media. All my friends had careers and the women I knew who stayed home with their kids never really had careers. Being a mom was their chosen career. I didn't feel as though I fit in anywhere. Years of doing this took a toll on my moxie because it caused a conflict with my identity. Fortunately, my husband at the time, recognized my struggle and suggested that I start doing some freelance writing to keep my mind challenged. For me, writing was a life saver. It helped to keep my mental state intact and kept that moxie flame burning. Like I said, I wouldn't have traded the experience of staying home and raising my kids for the world, but I wanted to show you what can happen when you are placed out of your element and in a situation that you may not be one hundred percent comfortable with. Being out of sorts for a time can cause a significant decrease in your moxie.

There are other things that can cause a loss of moxie such as staying in an unbearable job for too long or living in a place or situation that you really don't like. Serious issues such as mental illness and addiction can also diminish that big-old moxie flame. Traumatic events, which can cause PTSD, can also put a severe hurting on your moxie. Anything that takes a toll on you, also takes a toll on your moxie.

Now is a good time to stop reading and take a deep breath. I want you to take a moment to look back at your life and see if you can pinpoint the first time something happened, or someone said something to dull your moxie. Was it when you were still a child or was it when you were older? What kind of events happened that caused your light to diminish? How have your relationships been throughout your life? Have they been supportive and nurturing or have they been a painful experience for you? If you can, take a few moments and write down some of the biggest moxie killers you've had throughout your life. Words, events, situations, relationships, or whatever else comes to mind. In what way did these things diminish your moxie? Describe in one word how you feel about them now. Angry? Hurt? Sad? I ask you to do this because it's important to understand what happened to your moxie and how it has affected you. It's also an opportunity to learn more about yourself, which is a big step in your healing process. Often, we don't realize how many things we've experienced in our lives that have helped to diminish our moxie. We honestly have no idea until we sit down and begin to put them on paper. Once we begin, it's as if we've opened the floodgates. The more that we get out of us, the quicker we heal, the brighter our moxie shines.

Losing your moxie is devastating to you as a person and to your spirit. When this happens, we shrink back into a shell, nothing more than a skeletal version of ourselves. A sliver of what used to be a bright being. We retreat to a state of insecurity and self-consciousness about who we are and then question what we were meant to do. We can even lose sight of our original purpose. I honestly believe that loss of moxie can lead to depression.

But I am here to tell you that loss of moxie doesn't have to be permanent. That moxie, or that bright flame we were born with, is still there. Sure, it may have dimmed, or even given the appearance of being snuffed out, but trust me, it's there. It may be nothing more than a glowing little red ember, but it's there. Nurture that red ember and its glow will become brighter. Soon a flame will appear. Once burning, that flame will increase in size until it once again fills your entire being.

Losing your moxie is temporary. It will come back, but not on its own. You must reclaim it.

And it won't be easy. But last time I checked, nothing worth having, is ever gotten easily. Reclaiming your moxie means that you're going to have to do some work. You're going to have to roll up those sleeves and get a little dirty. You're going to have to reach deep inside yourself to understand why you lost it, heal old wounds, and then take it back. I say take it back, because it's rightfully yours and it was essentially stolen from you.

But now that you know that—now that you understand that it is rightfully yours—now is the time to take it back. And once you take it back, and realize what you've been missing all these years, you will never allow anyone to take it away from you ever again.

It's time to reclaim your moxie.

Not sure how to do it? Maybe a little scared?

Come, take my hand. Follow me and I'll show you how.

Be Prepared to Make Some Changes

Throughout this book I will be talking about some words or phrases that you may not be familiar with such as energy levels and vibrational frequencies. As someone who studies metaphysics, which includes the law of attraction, I believe that we have the ability to use our mind to transfer thoughts into energy and manifest things through this process. Yes, it sounds very hocus-pocus—I get that—but our thoughts are energy. Our brain waves are energy. Everything about us is energy. But there's more to it, so this is where I ask you to be open-minded. Each of us operate at various energy levels or vibrational frequencies. It's like channels on a radio or television. When you're tuned into the sports channel, you get sports. When you're tuned into the movie channel, you get movies. I'm oversimplifying things, but that is pretty much how things work with the law of attraction and universal energy. If you wanted to watch a great movie, you would not tune in to CNN, because all you would get is news. If you wanted to watch the Super Bowl, you would not tune in to HGTV, because you would get nothing but shows about decorating houses. If you want something specific you need to tune into the proper channel in order to get it. We all have vibrational frequencies and if we are to attract something that we want, then we need to operate at those frequencies.

When you lose your moxie, it can affect every area of your life. Because you are not operating at your maximum or peak state, your energy or vibrational level, is greatly diminished, and you begin to operate at a lower vibrational frequency. This lower frequency is not good for your moxie, because when your frequency is low you attract things that are also at a lower frequency. I'm not saying that they are always bad things, but they are certainly things that you would not want if you were operating at a higher frequency.

Suppose you decided to go on vacation. You love going on vacation. You visit the finest resorts and get VIP treatment wherever you go. So, you pack your suitcase with those new pink flops, lots of sunscreen, and head to the airport. When you get off the plane, instead of taking you to the Palm Island Resort and Spa which boasts five restaurants and three pools, the taxi driver takes you to the Blue Water Beach Motel which is located next to a hotdog stand and has a really cool sprinkler in the back of the property. There may be nothing wrong with the Beach Motel, but this is not the treatment you're used to or feel you deserve. This vacation is not up to your standards. The frequencies don't match.

This is where the law of attraction comes into play, and trust me, this shit is real. What you focus on, or put out in the way of frequencies, you get back. When you are not operating at your highest frequency because your moxie has been beaten down, you will not attract things of a higher frequency. You need to reclaim your moxie, raise your standards, and raise your frequency in order to attract things that you rightfully deserve in this life. There has been a great deal written about the law of attraction that can be readily found on the internet and books. I've also included some information in the resource section at the end of this book if you want to read more about it.

Let's use intimate relationships as an example. When you don't believe that you are good enough, or that you don't deserve a great relationship, you won't get one. And before you say, "Uh, Karen, everyone wants a good relationship," let me clarify—it's not about saying what you want, it's about believing what you are worthy of. You may say you are worthy, but, if there is the tiniest bit of doubt inside you, then your frequency will continue to remain at a lower vibration. If you don't believe you are worthy of wonderful things in your life, then you won't have them.

Have you ever been at a low point in your life and met someone who ended up being incredibly wrong for you? You may have thought that they were right at the time because your vibrational frequencies were low and that is what you were attracting. It may not have been a match made in heaven, but more likely a match made by frequency. As you begin to raise your frequencies, in the form of increased moxie, you will find that the person who you attracted at your lower frequencies is probably not the same person that you would want at your higher frequencies. Like attracts like. If you're feeling low and broken, that is often what you will attract. That is why I suggest holding off on relationships if you're going through a difficult time. Start reclaiming your moxie and then set to attract the right person in your life. In fact, you won't even have to do any hard work. The right person will appear. The standards you accept when you are operating at fifty percent moxie level are not the same standards you accept at one hundred percent moxie level.

And while we're on the subject of attraction, let me just make this clear. Stop telling yourself that all you ever get are jerks, bums, and losers as mates. When you tell yourself this crap, the energy goes out to the universe like it's some sort of special-order machine and pulls your order right back for you. *Order up! We've got a customer on earth who is telling people that she always ends up with some loser. Okay, Mister Universal Energy, I see that she's single again. Let's make this happen.* If you are intent on getting your moxie back, I'm begging you to stop this self-deprecating bullshit and set the intention that really good things are going to happen to you, including having great people enter your life. It's time to start telling yourself that an incredibly awesome person is out there and can't wait to meet you.

It's all about setting intention. You will attract the kind of things in your life that you ask for or say you get. Nothing more. Nothing less. Here's a perfect example. One day I happened to be listening to an audiobook by Jen Sincero, one of my favorite authors, and I almost fell over as she described how she always gets premium parking spots. *Wait a minute! I thought I was the only one this happened to!* So, here's the deal. I always get great parking spots. Those six words have actually become one of my mantras. It's a given. It just always happens. I tell everyone I know that I get really great parking spots. I say it and I believe it, so it is. It's to the point that everyone prefers I do the driving if we're heading out, especially if it's to the mall or a crowded parking lot. I just set the intention when I'm driving that I always get good parking spots, and low and behold, I do. So, if you're looking to get great parking spots like me, Jen, and everyone else who does, then start setting your intentions and watch how things begin to change. By the way, this shit doesn't just work for parking spots—it works for lots of other things that you want to manifest in your life. Just set the intention.

I talk a lot about intentions and vibrational frequencies because it's important in attracting many wonderful things in your life, including the right partner, but what happens if you are already in a relationship and your vibrational frequency changes? If you are currently in a not-so-great relationship, and are reclaiming your moxie, I warn you that there may be some rough roads ahead, because your frequency will rise and there is a good chance that your significant other's will remain the same. This often happens, and if it does, be prepared for some possible tension in the relationship, especially if your partner is not into change or has no interest in raising their own frequency. When frequencies rise, your standards will rise. Whatever behavior or traits that were acceptable to you before may not be so acceptable to you now. You might even wake up one day, look over at that person, and think to yourself *what was I thinking*? You may decide that this person is no longer right for you because of the differences in vibrational frequencies. When you raise your frequency and reclaim your moxie, there is a monumental shift in the very essence of your being. It can be scary for your partner because there is something much different about you. Something has changed, and they have a feeling that many more changes could be right around the corner. If you are lucky enough to be in a good relationship while you are reclaiming your moxie, then your partner will be cheering you on. Your reclaimed moxie will not be a threat to them. If it's a threat, then you got a problem, and need to re-evaluate your situation.

But the whole law of attraction thing is not just about intimate relationships. Operating at a higher frequency can attract other things in your life such as great friends, lots of opportunities, and abundance. Remember what I said earlier, like goes to like. When you are at your peak state, peak things come your way because they are attracted to you and the frequency is the same. When you are not operating at your peak state, you are attracting things that are not so great for you. Honestly, who wants that?

You can't stay stuck where you are, continue doing what you've been doing, and expect a different outcome than you've had. In order to reclaim that moxie, you're going to have to do some things that are going to be uncomfortable for you. They may be things that you used to do, but stopped doing, so they are no longer familiar to you. They may be things that you've never done before in your life. But you will need to do them if you want change. We start to reclaim our moxie when we begin to grow into our true authentic selves. You know who that is—it's that person way down, deep inside of you who wants to come out and shine for this world to see and appreciate.

Being small and bowing to the will of others has made you content in some ways. You've accepted their limiting beliefs as your own. You have traded in your growth for complacency. You've spent all these years deciding not to rock the boat for fear of being looked at differently. You've followed the status quo without speaking up and saying, "That's not working for me. I'm different. I've got too much to offer this world to allow it to sit quietly inside me." You know that somewhere deep inside you there is an ember that still burns and yearns to have you fulfill your purpose on this planet. An ember that has the potential to grow into a magnificent flame, a flame that burns so bright, it will never again be dimmed or snuffed out, because you will no longer allow it to.

So, we're going to shake some things up a little, or a lot, depending on how much moxie has been lost and how badly you're willing to get it back. You're going to have to reach outside your comfort zone because that's the only way that growth will ever occur. There may be times when you feel like you will only be able to take small steps, and that's okay. There may be times when you end up taking incredibly large leaps. Go with what stretches you as a person. Go with what will help you grow. But, remember to be gentle with yourself. Healing can take some time. You didn't lose your moxie overnight, and it won't be overnight that you get it back.

I'm going to ask you to do some hard, but incredibly healing stuff throughout this book. How much you decide to do, and to what degree, is entirely up to you. If I were an attorney, I might insert a disclaimer here saying something like, "reader takes all risks, blah, blah, blah," but this truly is your journey. As much as I want to reach in, grab that moxie, and give it back to its rightful owner—you, I can't. This is something that only you can do. Only you can do the healing necessary to get it back.

So what changes might you have to make in order to reclaim your moxie? Well, letting go of your limiting beliefs is one of them. I'm going to ask you to let go of a lot of things throughout this book, such as pain, anger, and fear, but I believe that letting go of these things will be like removing incredible weights from your soul. I'm also going to ask you to make some changes. Some of these changes may be easy and some of them may be really hard. These changes might include your attitude, your job, your friends, your relationships, and anything else you believe is holding you back from being your best and true self. Understand that sometimes we must let go of some things in order to gain more.

As I've said before, you are going to have to venture outside your comfort zone to grow and reclaim that moxie. I ask you to read this book with an open mind and an open heart. I may ask you to do some things that are not very conventional. I may ask you to do some things that you might find incredibly difficult and painful, but I ask you to do these things because I love you. Yes, you read that right. I love you. I have been you. I have been where you are. I have felt beaten down, lonely, depressed, and fearful. I have felt incredible pain and deep sadness throughout my entire being. There were days that I didn't want to get out of bed because I didn't have the energy or desire. Days where even taking a breath seemed to be too much of an effort. Days where I just wanted to close my eyes and never open them again. Days where I had sunk into such a deep dark abyss, I didn't think I could ever return from it.

But I knew, just as you know, that somewhere deep inside of me, there was something still there, even if it was just barely there. I knew that there was something that had the potential to burn bright, and if I could just figure out a way to get it back, my magnificent light would shine. I knew that if I could find the way, then I could help others. Finding the way, did not come easy. It came as a result of change. Some of that change was so incredibly difficult to make I wondered if it were even possible. Some of it meant that I had to abandon core beliefs that I held onto throughout most of my life. But I did it. I made the changes and reclaimed my moxie.

And you will too. Trust me. When no one else believes in you, know that I do. When you wonder if you will ever be healed, know that I was, and continue to be, more and more each day. You are not alone. Ever. I am with you each step of the way. Promise.

Now, let's go get some moxie!

Let Go of Pain and Trauma

*M*oxie cannot thrive if you continue to suffer through pain and trauma from the past. It is important that you begin the healing process. We will talk more about specific healing practices later, but right now, I just want you to focus on beginning your journey of healing. One of the first steps you need to take involves letting go of any pain and trauma that you've experienced throughout your life. I know it's hard. It involves releasing hurt, pain, anguish, and a whole bunch of other fucked-up emotions brought about by things that happened to you or even things that you've done. This is the first step to reclaiming your moxie. We lug our past around like an old worn out suitcase not realizing that the weight of it prevents us from moving into the present and the future. It's like we have a chain wrapped around our ankle which does not allow us to move away from our horrible experiences. Many people who hold onto pain and trauma end up holding onto tangible items also. This is where hoarding occurs. I know letting go of pain and trauma can be difficult. For some of you, it may be the most difficult step of all, but it is also critical if you are going to move forward. You've got to take that big scary first step.

I know you have struggled. I know you are tired. I know these things because I have been there. I know you have days where you don't even feel like getting up or taking another breath. The weight of it can feel unbearable, but trust me when I say, you are not alone. There are many people just like you who struggle and are tired too. You may feel isolated—like you're standing on the outside of the playground, with your fingers poking through and wrapped around the fence, watching everyone else having fun and just going about their lives—but, trust me, there are many others standing outside that fence, looking in, just like you. I want you to know that this feeling is only temporary. It's a small blip on the screen of your life. There is so much out there waiting for you and it is well within your grasp. You just have to want it and start heading towards it. Know that you were placed on this earth for a purpose and that you have an incredible gift to share with us. Don't worry about what has happened in the past. There's no need to look back because you are no longer heading in that direction. It's time to start living in the present and looking forward to your future.

Please understand that your past does not define you. I'm not sure why we feel the need to hold onto it so tightly. We really need to release it, but we just won't allow that to happen. It's difficult to understand why we are so hard on ourselves. We get so bogged down in our past, and keep turning back to look at it, but while we're looking back on the past, we're not focusing on the present or on our future. And that, my friend, is where we need to be. Never mind the things you've done in the past or what others have done to you. Never mind the events that have occurred. Wallowing in them only keeps the wounds open and ultimately prevents them from healing. Let it go. When we no longer allow the past to control us, and we are able to overcome the bullshit associated with it, we start to see freedom in the present and open ourselves to incredible opportunities ahead.

In order to heal, one thing you're going to have to overcome is the blame that you've been throwing on others all these years. This is par- amount for letting go of pain and beginning the process of healing. That's not to say that other people have not been the cause of some terrible shit that happened to you. That's not what I mean. I mean that you are no longer going to spend the rest of your life focusing on that person or event. It doesn't matter anymore. What was done, is done. Stop focusing on it, because it's preventing you from moving forward with your life, your light, and your purpose. Anyone who caused you pain or trauma will be dealt with as only the universe (or who I like to call Madam Karma) sees fit. Trust me, she can be one mean bitch and I would not want to get in the middle of that mess. Let her handle it.

And no, you don't have to see her in action to know it took place. Don't focus your energy wondering if she took care of the rotten bastard who did you wrong. Let it go. Trust that it is taking place and it is no longer your worry. It's time to take it off your plate, my love, because you will now have more awesome stuff to think about as you're reclaiming that moxie.

And while we're on the subject of blame, here's something you might not have thought about. You're going to have to stop blaming your- self. Yes, you read that right. Stop blaming yourself for stuff that's happened in your life. Look, it's okay to be accountable, and accept responsibility, for any part you may have played in how your life turned out, but for God's sake, stop holding yourself to a higher degree than you would have held anyone else. Here's a news flash for you, my love, you are not infallible. None of us are, yet we're quick to beat the crap out of ourselves for stupid things that we've done, or that we've allowed to happen in our lives, when we'd be offering a cupful of compassion for anyone else who made the same mistakes. It's time to take a break from beating yourself up.

And please don't blame yourself for being you. We tend to blame ourselves even when people take advantage of us. We are told that we're too nice. Too trusting. And we actually believe this bullshit. It's as if we're somehow at fault for the actions of the deceitful, unscrupulous people in this world. So, let me make myself clear. There is nothing, and I mean absolutely nothing, wrong with being a nice person. There is nothing wrong with trusting other people. That is how we should be. I am here to tell you that you are not at fault because some asshole took advantage of you and fuck the person who says you are. Do not change who you are. Do not allow others to change who you are. You just keep being your incredibly authentic self. There's nothing wrong with that.

I also want you to stop blaming yourself for the difficult decisions you've made throughout your life and accept them for what they are. Decisions. Good or bad. We all make them—both good and bad. Some of those decisions have led to beautiful things in our lives, and others have led to a real mess. It's okay to make both kinds. It shows that you're one of us beings who occasionally make mistakes. Once again, stop blaming yourself just because things didn't turn out the way you had expected. Know that you have learned something from every one of those bad decisions you've made along the way. It's time to move past kicking yourself over those bad decisions. So here are some sentence starters that you're going to start eliminating from your life as of right now.

I should've…

Had I known…

I wish I would've…

Why did I…

Why didn't I…

If I knew then...

Most people say that hindsight is 20/20, but I always say that it's 50/50. We assume that if we made a different decision or took a different path, we would with absolute certainty, know what the outcome would have been, and that it would have turned out better than it did. I don't subscribe to that. I believe we *think* we know what the outcome would have been, but we're never one hundred percent sure, so stop telling yourself you should have zigged instead of zagged. You know that old saying about crying over spilled milk? Well, that applies here, so stop crying. Just know that you've made the best decisions you could with the information you've had. It's time to stop kicking yourself over the choices you've made. We can't predict the future. The things we think will turn out fine, don't always, and the things we're not always sure of often turn out just fine. Stop being so hard on yourself.

You need to understand that one page does not write your whole book. Heck, it doesn't even write a chapter, so stop beating yourself up over stuff from the past. The pain and trauma you've experienced throughout your life has made you who you are today in both good ways and bad. There are so many wonderful things waiting for you right now, and in the future, if you can just let go of the past. Forget about the old pages filled with crap. Turn that page because a new chapter begins today. You are going to have some incredibly moxie-licious chapters to write in your book of life, and I can't wait to read them.

Do whatever it takes to get past your past. If you need to cry to make that happen, then sit yourself down and have that big old cry. Cry until you can't cry anymore, then release it. If you'd rather let out a big blood-curdling scream, then do that. Let out whatever emotion helps you to get beyond it. Getting beyond it means that you will finally close the door on the past, enjoy every moment of the present, and start looking forward to your future, and that my friend, is really where you need to be. The present and the future is where moxie shines the best.

So how do we remove the awful pain from the past? If it's bad enough, and you don't think you can do it on your own, then you may want to seek professional help. I talk more about that later in this book. Another thing you can do is visual imagery. One of the practices I suggest to my clients is to imagine all the pain and trauma from the past being pulled away from your body and into a big glass ball several feet in front of you. Then, visualize that glass ball shattering into a million pieces. As all those pieces break up, imagine them being whisked away and back out into the universe, because that energy no longer serves you. Another suggestion is to write about the painful and traumatic events you've experienced on paper and then set it on fire (in a safe place, of course) to symbolize the past and any associated pain being removed from your present and future. Know that what is in your past is over. It cannot hurt you anymore and you must be able to move away from it in order to help that moxie come back to its rightful vibrancy. If it takes a little while for the process to happen, that's okay. Some things take time. Be gentle and patient with yourself as you move through the process.

You need to close the door on the pain and trauma from your past if you want to heal. You can't stand in the doorway with one foot in the past, and the other foot in the present, going back and forth between the two sides. It's like the squirrel, running back and forth on the road, not deciding which side to be on. You know how that ends. Don't be a flat squirrel. Step out of that doorway and close the door—for good. You are safe now. Hold sacred space and know that you are loved by this incredible universe and are worthy of all the good things that this life has to offer. Let me say that again. You are worthy. Allow the pain and trauma from your past to become distant memories and know that these memories will continue to fade as you reclaim your moxie.

No More Scaredy Cats

*F*ear, anxiety, and worry are controlling emotions that can stop us dead in our tracks. These guys can take us on a wild fantasy ride, where we run away to scary places deep within our minds, while imagining the god-awful worst that could possibly happen. Our hearts start to race, and we spend many sleepless nights worrying about endless terrifying possibilities. These emotions present big challenges for us and our moxie, because once we allow them to control us, they essentially shut us off to any positive energy or abundance that might come our way. Think of these things as big energy roadblocks slamming down around you in all directions.

And for what purpose?

Let's face it, most of the things we worry about never even actually happen. I once heard a statistic that over 80% of the things we worry about never come to fruition. We play out all the different scenarios in our heads, and get ourselves worked up into such a frenzy, that we've already decided the outcome before anything even happens. Fear, anxiety and worry lead to stress. And stress is a killer. In fact, it is one of the biggest contributors to major health problems such as high blood pressure and heart disease. It didn't start out that way. In fact, when we were all just hanging around in our caves many thousands of years ago, stress was all about fight or flight. Stress helped us to make quick decisions based on our safety and preserving our life, but these days stress is not so much about being in peril as much as it's about worry and anxiety over everything in our daily lives.

So, what happens when we stress out? Well, funny you should ask. You see, there are all kinds of biochemical reactions that occur in your body on a daily basis. When it comes to stress, these biochemical reactions can really take a toll on the body. First, you have an overproduction of cortisol which contributes to high blood pressure, mood swings, fatigue, sleeplessness, and muscle weakness. Oh, and for those of you who worry about your weight, here's a little secret— your high cortisol levels are actually helping you to gain weight and keep the weight on. Stress does more damage to us physically than any other thing I can think of. I've seen one statistic stating that up to 75% of visits to a doctor are actually stress related.

So, what do we do? We worry, get all stressed out, can't sleep and have difficulties with our usual routine, so we go to the doctor, who in turn prescribes sleeping pills or anti-anxiety medication to "take the edge off." Then we end up feeling like we're zombied out because we have become numb to life's simplest situations. Oh, and let's not forget the various side effects of those drugs which can even include suicidal tendencies. Trust me, not everything in an amber bottle makes you well. Sometimes it can make you worse. We spend most of our time, energy, and money treating the symptoms without examining the root cause. If we can figure out the root cause, then we can fix the problem, which is a whole lot better than treating the symptoms. It's like trying to put a band-aid on a gushing artery. I don't care how many band-aids you put on it, unless you get that artery sutured, you're going to bleed out.

Look, I realize that we live in a society where stress comes at us from all angles. It certainly is a lot more stressful today than I can remember growing up. I'm not sure if the internet is responsible for the higher levels of stress or just that our routines have changed significantly over the years, but I do know that we, as a society, need to get a handle on it, or we're all going to get sick and die early deaths.

Tackling fear, anxiety, and worry are going to be big challenges for many of you. Hell, they can still be very big challenges for me at times, but you've got to figure out a way to decrease your stress level so that you can get healthier and allow that awesome energy of abundance to flow through and around you. I understand that it's impossible to totally eliminate these emotions from our lives, but we need to figure out a way to keep them to a minimum.

When I was going through my divorce I would wake up in the middle of the night, just wracked in fear and worry. I don't think I can even explain what the fear and worry were about. All I knew is that I had it. I would think about every facet of my life and start to worry about things going wrong. Dumb things that didn't even matter. But having this fear and worry got me into a horrible pattern where I began to stress about everything. One of the biggest things I stressed over was money. How to make it. How to spend it. How to make it last. It wasn't until my decision to learn about, and practice mindfulness, that I was freed from unnecessary worry and anxiety. For those of you who don't know about mindfulness, have no fear, I discuss it later in this chapter and offer some resources at the end of this book.

Many people spend their lives wondering *What if?*

These are two very scary words.

What if it doesn't work out? What if I'm wrong? What if I fail?

I have found that we spend so much of our time worrying about the "what ifs" that it stops us from moving forward and enjoying life. It stops us from making plans. It stops us from feeling good. These two words get our hearts pounding and paralyze us with fear. They steal our focus from being positive and force us into being negative.

How many times have we asked ourselves *what if*, and automatically assumed the answer was negative? How much time did we needlessly worry about something that might never actually happen? It's time to stop worrying.

So, let's start changing things around with the *what ifs*.

What if everything turned out just fine? Then what would you do?

What if you took a chance and it all worked out for you?

What if things went your way?

Positive goes to positive and negative goes to negative. Don't waste another moment of your life worrying about the "what ifs." Take your steps. Plan your course. Make your decisions. What happens after that, happens, and trust that you will be guided from there. Begin to believe that you are worthy of great things and that everything will turn out okay. So, stop worrying and start living.

I'm not going to tell you to just relax, because if you're anything like me, hearing those words will only piss you off. The person who tells you to just relax is probably the same person who tells you to smile when you're just sitting there minding your own business. I don't like those people. Telling someone to relax when they are worried about something really does nothing to calm them down or reduce their anxiety. It also does nothing to validate the feelings they are having at that moment. It's not so much about relaxing; it's more about how you respond to stress, real or imagined. People who struggle with fear, anxiety, and worry need tools to help them cope with these emotions, and I'm all about helping people find the right tools. To better cope with these emotions you need to make a few slight changes to your brain and the way you think.

I know, it's easier said than done, so I'm going to give you some help here. Remember earlier I said that I was going to ask some unconventional things of you? Well, here's one. I want you to start meditating. For those readers who already do, I'm feeling pretty pumped-up proud of you. For those readers who don't, it's time to start, because this shit's going to make a difference in your life. Look, we can't go getting our moxie back when we're acting like scaredy-cats and worry-warts all the time. We've got to get beyond this stuff, so trust me that I know what I'm talking about.

Meditation is one of the best ways to overcome fear, anxiety and worry. It's also good for your health. Research has shown that adding meditation to your routine may reduce high blood pressure, headaches, insomnia, and even aid in improving your memory. Meditation also invokes a relaxation response in your body which can help in the healing process. Some famous people who have practiced meditation on a daily basis include Ellen DeGeneres, Michael Jordan, Katy Perry, Clint Eastwood, Madonna, Paul McCartney, and Oprah Winfrey. It's funny how, when you mention meditation to most people, their immediate response is, "I could never sit still for that long and not think." Well, I'm here to tell you that meditation does not have to be done cross-legged for hours without using a brain cell. There is no right or wrong way to meditate. It is an incredibly personal experience and each person has to seek out the method that works best for them.

I often hold a class called Meditation for the Wine and Beer Crowd. I call it that because it conjures up a totally different mindset for people who don't think they could ever meditate. In this class I am able to dispel some of the myths people have about meditation. I tell people, that according to the National Science Foundation, we have anywhere from 12,000 to 60,000 thoughts running through our brains on any given day, so don't sweat it if one or two should sneak in during a meditation session. Trust me, they will. When they do, simply acknowledge them, and get back on track without beating yourself up. Meditation is a judgement-free zone.

Meditation is like buying a pair of sunglasses. You have to try on different styles to see which looks the best. If one pair doesn't make you look fabulous, then there are plenty of others you can try. Don't be discouraged. Just keep trying different types of meditation until you find the one that works best for you. There is guided meditation, non-guided meditation, and even mindful meditation. I have listed several resources in the back of this book if you want to get more information.

So, when it comes to meditation, basically here's what you do. Sit your ass down, preferably someplace quiet. Don't give me some lame excuse that you couldn't find a quiet spot in your house if your life depended on it. Then sit your ass down in your car. See how quickly we fixed that one for you? Next, you're going to ground yourself. I want you to picture some tether or anchor coming from your spine and traveling deep into the center of the earth. I call this your grounding cord and it can be anything you want. Some people picture tree roots. Some people picture a rope. Hell, I've even heard one woman talk of picturing a spin mop to ground her to the earth. Hey, to each their own. My own grounding cord is a beam of golden light that I sit on top of. I'm not sure why I chose that, it just happened to come to me. Don't overthink it. There are no wrong grounding cords.

Ok, now that you've sat your ass down, and figured out your grounding cord, now is the time to simply shut up, close your eyes and just think about…nothing. Oh boy, here's where I start to lose most people. Ok, so if your mind won't let you think about nothing (it eventually will, it just takes some practice) there are some things you *can* think about. You can focus on the breaths that you're taking. Focus on each one as you breathe in and then breathe back out. Just focus on those slow breaths. Breathe in. Breathe out. Breathe in. Breathe out. You could also try saying a mantra as you meditate. A mantra is a word or phrase that you repeat over, and over, and over, and well, you get the picture. You can pick a simple word like *gratitude* or *abundance*, or a phrase like *Universal energy flows through me.* Hell, you can even say *I love my cat* if you want. It doesn't matter. Just keep saying it in your mind over and over again. Do whatever keeps you in the zone for ten minutes or so. Another way to meditate is to mindfully focus on each part of your body, starting with your toes, and continue all the way up to your head. How does each body part feel? Is there tingling? Difference in temperature? I often use this type of meditation to help me fall asleep some nights. I don't think I've ever made it past my hips to be honest with you before I'm sound asleep.

Meditate twice a day. That's all it takes to begin the process of elim-inating fear, worry and anxiety from your mind and your life. We're talking twenty minutes a day, total. What's that? You don't have an extra twenty minutes a day to meditate? You're way too busy as it is now? Ok, so here's where I'm going to be a bit of a hard-ass and tell you that if you don't scroll through all the dumb shit on Facebook, Instagram, Twitter and whatever other social media you use to catch up on the latest political or animal memes, you'll find the time. The time is always there. It's how you choose to use it that makes the dif-ference. Decide on your priorities. If you want your moxie, or any-thing else bad enough, you will find the time. You will do whatever it takes.

Keep meditating twice a day. As I said before, start with ten minutes for each session. If ten minutes seems like too much, then start with five. Eventually build up to more time during each session. It's kind of like a running a marathon. You wouldn't get up on the morning of the Boston Marathon and decide to run it, would you? No, you would spend a great deal of time training for it, especially if you've never run that long of a distance before. You would start out by running short distances until you got that mastered. Then you would slowly build up to longer distances until you were able to run that mara-thon. Well, there's no difference here when it comes to meditation. You start off small and slowly build your way up to a longer session. Once you start making meditation part of your daily practice, you'll find that you feel better as a whole. Things won't bother you like they used to. You'll also find yourself looking forward to your meditation sessions because it's a block of time dedicated to no one else but you.

So, we've spent some time talking about meditation, but if you want a deeper process to help you with fear, worry and anxiety, then I implore you to consider mindfulness training. This one's a game-changer, folks. No, scratch that—this ones' a life-changer if you can commit to learning the process. I know mindfulness has become a real buzzword over the past several years, to the point where I feel like the overuse of the word has started to create a real disservice to this incredible process. People only see the very tip of the mindfulness experience, but there is so much more than what is at the surface. Yes, being mindful is being in the moment. Yes, there are lots of mindful meditation tapes you can get to help you with your meditation. But mindfulness is a process that, when learned, can change the way you think and respond to things going on in your life.

Mindfulness is an incredible process that assists you with empowerment and allows you to experience freedom from fear, anger and anxiety (and whatever other crap that is getting in your head and not doing you any good). I cannot make this clear enough. Mindfulness takes you to a whole new level of the game. Mindfulness makes moxie grow substantially because it helps you to filter out all the nonsense in the background and to acknowledge the feelings that are going on in that moment. Once you can acknowledge them, you can better deal with them.

To truly appreciate mindfulness, you should consider enrolling in a course. I know of someone who offers a free eight-week mindfulness-based stress reduction (MBSR) course online. Yes, you read that right—Dave Potter, a retired psychotherapist and fully certified MBSR instructor, offers a free online course. Oh, look at that, I've just eliminated your *I don't have any extra money for a mindfulness course* excuse. I've listed information about the course on the resources page. Dave has done it all for you by providing the videos, worksheets and reading material. Taking this course will transform you, but in order for it to be effective, you've got to do the work and you've got to stick it out for the entire course. But if you do, I am telling you, it will totally change the way you view things in life, and it will help you deal with those emotions that are keeping you from reclaiming that moxie.

So why the big fuss about meditation and mindfulness? How exactly is this supposed to help you? Well, it's all about neuroplasticity. This is the brain's incredible ability to rewire or reorganize itself to adapt to new thought processes or situations. The brain can essentially alter itself by using different connections and neural pathways. Mindfulness and meditation are now being used frequently in many healthcare facilities, and research continues to evolve about the benefits of these two practices.

On a personal note, I credit these two practices with not only reducing stress and anxiety from my life, but also helping to relieve the pain from fibromyalgia, thus providing me with a better quality of life. If you are someone who suffers from anxiety or chronic pain, then I implore you to explore meditation and mindfulness. Stop wasting time. The sooner you put these practices into place, the better you will feel and the sounder you will sleep. Meditation and mindfulness are moxie builders because they help to alleviate stress, promote clarity, and allow you to focus on having a better life.

Anger

*A*nger is a powerful emotion and certainly has a place in your life as long as it promotes a positive change. Sometimes getting angry is the kick in the ass we need to get moving into a better situation. But when it begins to consume your life, then anger is probably causing you more problems than you realize, and there's only one solid piece of advice I can give you.

Get over it.

I don't care what it is. I don't care how bad it was. You cannot hold onto anger because it will eventually destroy you from the inside out. It will also keep you from that moxie that you're so desperately looking to reclaim. Freeing yourself from anger is incredibly liberating and allows your spirit to once again soar. I cannot stress this enough.

Are you still holding onto something that someone said or did to you way back from your past? Let's face it, there are plenty of jerks out there who intentionally, or unintentionally, just seem to piss people off. But let me tell you this. While you've held onto your anger all these years, those people have most likely moved on with their lives, and never even gave you a second thought. So, the way I see it, is that they are still controlling you. They still have a hold on you. Don't allow them to do it. I can guarantee that the anger and seething you've been holding onto is slowly consuming your soul. It anchors you to that particular place and time of the event and prevents you from moving on.

I'm amazed at how long people can remain angry. I know people, who when they talk about how they were wronged in some way, either by an ex-spouse or some other person in their life, talk about it with the same amount of emotion as if it just happened to them that morning. That same rage is still there. They've never moved beyond it. Their faces contort, their blood pressure goes through the roof, and their voices climb several decibels to the point of yelling. Over something that happened years ago.

Really?

They say, "I can't help it. When I think about it, it makes me mad," and then I say, "No, you definitely can help it, and you're ridiculous because your anger, and your body's response to the event, as if it's happening once again at this very moment, is causing lots of really ugly biochemical reactions inside of you." Come on people, how long are you gonna hold onto it?

And while we're on the subject of anger I'm going to ask you to stop holding onto your grudges. I've seen people hold onto grudges or not talk to people for years because they think they are "right." Really? Who cares? Let's think about this. What is more important in your life, to be right or to be happy? If it's to be right, then I can guarantee that you'll never be happy. Happy people, people who have joy, don't worry about making it a point to be right. They make it a point to have peace. They make it a point to have good relationships. They don't get bogged down in the stupid, petty bullshit because there are so many more important things to focus on. If you have allowed your ego and sense of being "right" to stop you from having a relationship with someone you love, then you're doing a big disservice to you and to them. Get over yourself. While you've been right, and held onto that energy, the clock has been ticking. How much wasted time has gone by? How many things did you lose out on because of pride? Let them be right. It's so insignificant. Make the choice to be happy.

Sadly, there are some people who just cannot move on from their anger and seek to be destructive with it. They have angry outbursts, stomp around, slam doors, and even stoop to giving people the silent treatment. If you're doing any of these things, then you might consider getting some therapy to figure out what the underlying issues are. Even the silent treatment is childish and immature. If you're the one giving people the silent treatment, it's time to stop and grow up. If you're the one getting the silent treatment, then maybe it's time to start hanging with people who no longer operate emotionally as children.

I'm not telling you to never be angry over stuff or the people who make your blood boil. What I am telling you, is to let out your scream, maybe wish them a really nasty stomach bug (although keep that Karma thing in mind) and move on. Let the anger go. Get it resolved in your head, your heart and your spirit. Move on from it.

If you are holding onto anger because you feel as though you've been wronged, treated badly or unjustly, then do something about it. Speak to that person to get it resolved. If that's not possible then look for a constructive outlet for that anger. You are not the only person in the world who has been treated badly or gone through bad situations. Others have too. By focusing on what has been done to you, by continuing to hold onto that anger, you stay in the role of victim.

You are not a victim. Moxie cannot thrive inside the victim. It cannot grow because it's being stifled. It cannot be reclaimed because it is still being taken by someone else.

You are the victor. You are the survivor. Own it.

Many people in this world have taken their hurt and anger and turned it into something good for others. Nancy Grace, a well-known television personality and champion of victim's rights, was 19 years old and on her way to becoming an English professor, when her fiancé was murdered. She used that anguish and anger to enroll in law school and become a prosecutor seeking justice for the victims who could not speak up for themselves. Her anger took criminals off the street and saved countless lives because of it.

John Walsh, whose young son Adam was kidnapped from a Florida mall and murdered, turned his anger and grief into co-founding the National Center for Missing & Exploited Children to help other parents and their children. He created the television show America's Most Wanted to help bring justice to the victims of crime. That show was responsible for helping law enforcement capture over 1,200 fugitives and enabling the safe return of more than 50 missing children.

There are countless others who don't make the celebrity list but have used their anger and grief to make a difference for others in this world. If they can do it, then so can you. Take that anger and channel it. Do something awesome and courageous with it. Are you a survivor of domestic abuse or child abuse? Turn that anger into action. Volunteer to help others in that same situation. Did someone speak badly or gossip about you? Then take a look at your own actions to make sure that you're not doing the same thing to others. Step up and say you're not going to be a part of it. Anger can be a powerful force of change in our lives if we make the decision to use it in that manner.

The emotion of anger has to be a balancing act inside our brains. We must seek to find a place between the out-of-control *I'm going to kill someone* rage-associated anger and the *I'm going to have a slow boil and let it eat at me until I explode* suppressive anger. Either one of these practices harms us as individuals, or our society as a whole. Our society has a big problem when it comes to anger and how to deal with it. We only have to turn on the news each day to understand this. There are two things I truly believe.

Kind people don't kill people.

Only hurt people, hurt people.

Try for a moment to imagine how much rage and hurt you would have to have in order to unload a barrage of bullets on people that you don't even know. To kill people who have done no harm to you. Imagine the anger. Imagine the pain. Is this really something you want in your life? Is this something you want your kids or the people around you witnessing?

Ok, so now you're thinking, *I'm not that angry, Karen. Geez, you're making me out to be some psycho just because I have some rage still in me from some shit that happened to me in the past.*

What I am telling you, is that rage is very good at hiding itself in each one of us. It can come out at the slightest of provocation and can easily cause an escalation if you allow it to. So, with that in mind, ask yourself the following.

When I see a post, tweet or something else on social media that really pisses me off, do I quickly respond with more anger by telling the person they're an idiot for having that opinion, or do I simply move on?

When some asshole rushes to get in the lane ahead of me while I'm driving or doesn't let me merge in front of them, do I lay on my horn as if I'm a freight train crossing a wide road, give them the finger and scream obscenities at them, or do I simply let them be their asshole self and allow them to move on from my life?

Sorry, I don't want to hear *but he did, she did, or they did* because it doesn't matter. What really matters is what *you* do. It's how *you* respond to it. It's whether or not *you* allow *yourself* to be pulled into it. How many incidents of road rage happen because of escalation? How many simple arguments turn into long-standing family feuds because things get out of hand? Have we not learned anything since the Hatfields and the McCoys? We've all seen the Facebook posts that quickly get out of control because someone posts something that someone else doesn't agree with. Next thing you know, people are screaming at each other and calling each other names over the safety and security of a keyboard. I often wonder how many people would actually have the nerve to say those things to each other in person?

People who allow anger to control their lives often just don't know how to release that anger in a productive or constructive way. Frequently, there is some sort of pain inside them that they hold onto instead of letting go. Sometimes all they have to hold to is their anger. It's the only thing that drives them. If they let it go, they have nothing left, and that's really sad.

So how do you release anger when someone or something has done you wrong? There are several things you can try to release any anger that you have been carrying with you. The important thing is to get it released.

You can try envisioning a cord that ties you to that person or event. Where is that cord attached? Your wrist? Your ankle? Your waist? Your neck? Next, I want you to envision that cord stretched so tight that it prevents movement. It stops you from all the great things you want for your life. Feel that cord as it pulls at you. Feel how uncomfortable it feels. The weightiness of it. You struggle to move from it, but it just won't let go. You know that cord should not be part of you. You know that it is not part of all the good things you desire in your life. Acknowledge that it has been there for a long time and now it is time to move on from it. That person or event no longer holds you or controls you. See yourself cutting that cord or burning it with a beautiful gold beam of light, and in doing so, releasing the tension of the cord that once was between you and that person or event. Feel the instant release that occurs when that cord is no longer attached to you. What does that feel like? Freedom? Relief? Don't hold onto things you no longer need, because they are keeping you from things you deserve.

This next suggestion will definitely be more challenging for some people, but really offers the most growth when it comes to releasing anger. Have compassion. Oh, I know, this one is asking a lot of you, but as we've already said, hurt people, hurt people. Someone who causes pain is in a great deal of pain themselves. You, on the other hand, are reclaiming your moxie. You are experiencing tremendous personal growth and becoming your authentic self. You are in the process of becoming whole. And I'm sorry to have to tell you this, but part of this process is finding compassion for others. There is no "eye for an eye" thing going on here. Ugh, I hate when people cherry-pick the Bible to justify their actions, but that's a conversation for another day.

Lastly, as you go on through life, understand that not all anger is directed at you in response to something you did. When I coached political candidates on how to campaign door-to-door, one of the first things I told them was that during their travels, they might go to a door only to have someone scream at them and slam it in their face. I told them to not take it personally. Yeah, it's possible that they might hate politicians, but more likely, there's something else going on in their lives that you will never know about. They could have just been told by their spouse that they want a divorce. They could have just found out that they, or someone they love, has cancer. They could have just lost their job or gotten notice of their house being foreclosed on. It could have been a combination of things throughout the day building up and you just happened to be there at the moment of eruption. As that door slams, simply take a moment to take a deep breath, silently send them good thoughts and wish them well as you continue on your way.

This is the same advice I will give you when it comes to encountering anyone who seems to vent their anger on you or lash out. That

Facebook post or the asshole who cut you off? Just feel sorry for them or silently wish them well. Don't escalate it. Just. Let. It. Go. Trust me, if you can get this anger thing under control, you're going to sleep a whole lot better at night.

What do you do about people currently in your life who have anger issues? If you find that someone continually lashes out in anger, calmly, and I mean calmly, let them know that their behavior is unacceptable. If you acknowledge their anger, most often, you will find out the reason behind it. During my time as a local councilwoman, people would often come to my meetings, fuming about things. After listening to them yell, I would make it a point to acknowledge their feelings, "I can see you're very angry," I would say to them. I cannot tell you how many times they would say, "Yes, you're right, I am angry." But then something else happened. I could see the anger start to dissolve once I acknowledged their feelings. After that, they tended to give the reason for their anger in a much calmer tone. Once I knew the reason, I could address it and help them. Hopefully, you can do the same with people in your life who have a great deal of anger. If not, then you may need to make some decisions as to whether you want this person to continue to be in your life. You may have to love this person, and that may include family members, from a distance. We need to accept that we cannot help everyone. We can only help the people who want to be helped, and that includes ourselves.

Sometimes we get angry because of circumstances that happened in our lives. We are angry because things didn't turn out the way we had hoped or planned. We are angry because bad things have happened to us, and we think they shouldn't have, because we're good people. You have to understand that sometimes bad things happen to good people. Bad things also happen to bad people. Bad things happen to all people; it's just part of life. You are not being singled out. Stop taking it personally. Accept it for what it is and move on. People with moxie understand that during a lifetime, things will not always be perfect. Things will not always go the way they are planned. Release the anger and move forward with your life.

Remember we are on a mission to reclaim our moxie, and releasing things that no longer serve us, helps us to do that. Anger from the past is just that—something from our past that no longer serves us. When you learn to release your anger from the past, you will be amazed as to how quickly you can release it from the present. This is an example of how you begin to control your emotions instead of allowing them to control you. Free yourself from anger and open yourself up to all the good things that are coming your way.

It's not Failure, It's Research

Failure. It's a scary word and it prevents us from doing lots of great things in our lives. The fear of failure often keeps us from moving forward and taking chances or fulfilling our hopes and dreams. We're afraid to fail.

But, what if during all this time, we saw things differently when it came to failure? What if we saw failure in a whole new light? Would it change the way we look at things or even how we look at ourselves? If we saw failure as something else, something less scary, would it help us to move ahead, stop blaming ourselves for things gone wrong, and finally allow us to start enjoying our lives?

I spent many years working as a research scientist in the pharmaceutical field. Science is filled with failures. Scientists don't just walk into the lab, mix together a couple of ingredients, and come up with a new cure for a disease. It's an effort that takes years, sometimes decades, to accomplish. Unfortunately, for those who wait for a cure, it can sometimes feel like forever. Failure in the lab occurs during every single step of the process. You can't get away from it. It doesn't matter how much education you have, how much time or money you've spent on the project, or how many people are counting on it. Failure will occur. Guaranteed. In fact, failure is a result more guaranteed than success when it comes to research.

But here's the difference. Failure in science is expected. We see it so often, that we don't allow it to control us. We can't. For if it did, we would most certainly put away the beakers and walk out of the lab forever without ever looking back.

"That's why we call it research," is a phrase that gets said all day long in the lab when something goes wrong. To this day I still say this phrase to people, especially my children, when things don't work out the way we expect them to. You can't wallow around in the failure because it will consume you.

Now that doesn't mean that we are not highly disappointed by failures that occur in the lab. We strive to move forward. We want to help people get well. We continue to push for new discoveries. But the simple fact remains that we will see failure much more than we will see success.

No scientific success was ever gotten without failure.

None.

Nil.

Zero.

We would not have landed on the moon without failure.

We would not have organ transplants without failure.

We would not have the knowledge to test for diseases without failure.

We would not be flying a plane or driving a car without failure.

So, if this is the case, then why are people so hard on themselves when they are working on the great research project called Life?

Failure is a negative word we place upon ourselves as a punishment. The word we really should be using is opportunity, because that's what it is. Every hiccup, every obstacle, is an opportunity to learn and overcome a result we did not expect. And that's what failure is—a result we just did not expect.

Before we make something right, we need to understand where, or why, it went wrong. In no way is this a failure. It's a great opportunity to discover, and more importantly, showcase our skills to overcome a challenge. The more important thing is that we made the attempt, because without the attempt, we might never get the chance to learn something new, or even have the possibility of obtaining a result we expect. We need to stop being so hard on ourselves when we get a result that we didn't expect in life. The greatness is in making the attempt and learning along the way.

Project Life is filled with opportunities and paths. We stumble. We fall. We make decisions based on the information we know at that time. When things don't go the way we expect them to, it's not the end of the project. Make a new plan, overcome the obstacle, and learn from it. The project does still go on. It must.

Will you get some unexpected results?

Yes.

Is it the end of the world?

No.

Moxie doesn't know failure. It only knows that it must continue to try to find a way to make things happen. Don't be ashamed of failure. Hold your head up. Do not allow the snickers and sneers of small-minded people to keep you from taking repeated risks and steps. Keep failing until you succeed. History is filled with people who repeatedly took risks, only to fail multiple times before they finally saw success. Walt Disney was fired from a newspaper job because his editor told him that he lacked imagination. Theodor Seuss Geisel, most of us know him as Dr. Seuss, had his first book rejected 27 times before it was finally published. Sir James Dyson had 5,126 failed prototypes before getting that awesome vacuum just right. Steven King's best seller *Carrie* was rejected 30 times. Thomas Edison failed over 1,000 times before creating the light bulb. Bill Gates, the cofounder of Microsoft, experienced failure during his first business venture. And poor Abe Lincoln, was born into poverty, had two failed businesses, lost eight elections, and had a nervous breakdown, all before becoming president. Now, if that's not a show of moxie, I don't know what is.

Take a moment to make a list of the failures you've had in your life and then write down what you have learned from them. And don't tell me you haven't learned anything. There's always something to learn from every failure in our life, even if we've learned to not do the same thing all over again. See, those failures weren't for nothing. You experienced growth during those failures. You were essentially doing some research in Project Life. So, let's turn this bad-boy around. You weren't a failure. You were a researcher. You were a Project Life scientist. Hold your head high, you badass. You're starting to rock that moxie!

Get Help to be Healed

*R*eclaiming our moxie means that we are healing mentally, emotionally, spiritually, and even physically, but sometimes we need outside help in our healing process. Although it's great to be able to do it on your own, looking to others can actually help the process move a bit more smoothly, if not more quickly. I understand that seeking outside help in healing may put you outside of your comfort zone. You may feel weak because you can't do it on your own. You may feel embarrassed because you come from a place where people just don't "talk about those things" with others, but I encourage you to get help with your healing process, because we're not put on this planet to do things alone. We're here to help one another be the best we can be. Reclaiming your moxie means that sometimes we need to do things outside our comfort zone because that is when we start to experience the most growth.

It's amazing that we are so quick to get relief from any physical pain that we have, yet we are hesitant to get relief from any mental or emotional pain. Not long ago, I had the misfortune of going to the hospital emergency room because of the flu. I had been coughing so bad that my lungs were really causing me to be in a lot of pain. As I sat there in the examination room, my eyes settled on one of those pain charts. You know, the kind with the numbers under the faces? Zero is no pain with a smiley face. As the numbers go up the faces become more anguished. The last number, ten, was under a really scrunched up, painful face. My husband followed my stare and looked at the chart. He asked what my pain number was. I told him that it was an eight. "An eight? Really?" he asked.

"Yes, right now it's really bad. I prefer life when I'm feeling a zero or even a two. Although with my fibromyalgia it can sometimes go a little higher."

He cocked his head, and then asked, "Do you ever feel a ten?"

I thought about it, almost said no, and then changed my mind. "Yeah, occasionally I do, but that's usually when I'm dealing with my teenage son, Justin."

All kidding aside, I started to think about how we are encouraged to speak about our physical pain on a scale from one to ten, but no one ever asks us about our emotional or mental pain and where that sits on the same scale. If you see someone limping on the street, you might stop and ask if you can help them in any way, but people walk down the street every day, with emotional and mental pain that goes unnoticed by others because it can't be seen, and that's sad. Think about how different things would be if we could openly tell people our emotional or mental numbers so that people would know that we weren't feeling so good that day. Mental health carries a stigma in this country and I'm not sure why, but I do know that until we remove the stigma and address the issue, we will continue to see mass shootings and people lashing out in horrific ways. We need to be more proactive in making sure that people get the help that they need when they're not feeling so well. We need to remove the stigma. Seeking help is not weak, it's courageous.

If you feel that you want or need some help to get over some mental or emotional hurdles, then I encourage you to seek out some of the modalities I mention in this chapter and find one (or several) that will help you. The list certainly does not encompass all the modalities out there, just the few that I am most familiar with. Each of us must find our own path to healing, but once found, it can truly help us on our journey to reclaim our moxie. Healing is powerful. Don't deny yourself this process.

Therapy or Counseling

There are a number of therapists or counselors that can help you if you think you might need to travel down this road. Some people struggle with deep-seated trauma in their lives and the only way to resolve this is through therapy. Therapy helps people to uncover and unlock issues from their past. It can also help people find emotional resolution to issues that keep them from moving forward. Therapy can help people recognize behavioral patterns in their lives and help them to break these patterns. If you feel that you need a counselor or therapist to help you in the healing process, you can get recommendations from your insurance carrier or possibly your local mental health center. Mental health is something that gets overlooked in this country far too often. For some reason we're quick to run to a doctor when we have a physical ailment and want pain relief, but we continue to suffer in pain when it comes to our mental health. If you are struggling with pain from mental health issues, get the help that you deserve. Get the healing you are worthy of.

Coaching

A coach is not a therapist. A coach is someone who helps to hold you accountable, can set up a plan or goals for you, and motivate you to reaching those goals. Coaches tend to work more on the here and now, and the future. As a coach, I can guide you through issues going on in your life, but if I believe that someone needs therapy, I will certainly refer them to someone who can handle that. I like to think that my job is to motivate and challenge people to success, whatever their version of success may be. I have coached people to lose weight, become more centered and grounded, and get through some of life's challenges including illnesses. I have coached candidates running for political office by keeping them focused on their campaigns and message to voters. I have coached business owners on how to increase sales and run successful businesses. Some coaches specialize in specific areas while other coaches have broader practices. My coaching practice is geared towards transformation and success which are totally defined by each client. Coaches are important in that they help people stay focused on what they are looking to achieve. And yes, even coaches have coaches. I personally have used business and personal development coaches. If you are looking to make some massive changes in your life, need help meeting a particular goal, or even being held accountable, then a coach would be a good investment.

Holistic Work

Meditation and mindfulness are two modalities that we've touched on so far, but there are countless others. Many of them fall under complementary and alternative medicine (CAM) which encompass an integrative approach to wellness. The National Institutes of Health (NIH) now has a CAM division to study the effectiveness of different holistic modalities such as acupuncture and energy healing on various illnesses and medical conditions. I will speak about energy healing because that is what I am most familiar with and practice. Here, once again, I ask you to have an open mind.

Energy Healing

When I start talking to people about energy healing, I am sometimes met with a roll of the eyes, like I'm a lunatic who was just beamed in from another planet. I can see their eyes glaze over as they shut down the process of listening to me. Some people even politely smile as they start looking for the nearest exit. Then I casually mention that I spent seventeen years as a pharmaceutical scientist. Well, you should see the difference in their reactions. Their ears suddenly perk up, and all of a sudden, they're interested in hearing a bit more about this energy healing stuff. Five minutes ago, I was just your average nutcase rambling on about biofields and chakras. Now all of a sudden, I'm a credentialed somebody who might just know a thing or two about science and energy.

So, here's the deal. If you think we're all solid beings, you're in for a real surprise. We are actually a bunch of bouncy, vibrating balls of energy. I know that doesn't sound very scientific coming from a former scientist, but I really wanted to spare you the quantum physics lecture. We are energy. Actually, everything is energy once things are broken down to the smallest level. And everything energy has an energy field.

So, let's take a quick look at our body. We see a whole human being, which looks pretty solid, but if we break it down, we'll see that we are not as solid as we first thought. We are made up of organs and tissues. The organs and tissues are actually made up of millions of cells. Cells are made up of tiny molecules and molecules are made up of atoms. So, here's the deal—atoms are made up of vortices of energy that are continually vibrating. As I said before, we are energy.

Everything is energy. Don't believe me? How do you think your radio plays music in the car? How do you think your emails get from one person to another? How can I make a call to someone across the country, or the world for that matter, with my cellphone? It's energy. Just because we don't see it or can't feel it, doesn't mean it's not there. Think about electricity. Think about Wi-Fi.

One of my favorite movies is *City of Angels* with Meg Ryan and Nicholas Cage. In this movie, Cage plays an angel and Ryan plays the role of a heart surgeon. At one point they are talking about a patient who died during surgery and she can't seem to understand it. Cage tells her that the patient still lives, just not the way she thinks. She tells him, "I don't believe in that," to which he responds, "Some things are true whether you believe in them or not." That is the point I am trying to make about energy healing. Just because we don't fully understand something, doesn't mean that it doesn't exist. There are many things that exist, especially in the world around us, that science has not yet fully explained.

Energy healing is the process of working with a person's biofield and channeling energy to go where it is needed. It helps to balance a person's physical, mental, emotional and spiritual well-being. Oh, and it feels pretty damn good, too. So good, that it's not unusual for people to fall asleep while it's being done.

During an energy healing session, the recipient lies fully clothed on a massage table, although it can also be done on a chair; whatever is most comfortable for the client. The practitioner assesses and evaluates the recipient's energy field, detecting imbalance which can be felt in the form of temperature or sensation changes. The procedure can be done with hands on or off the body. The recipient is fully aware of what is going on at all times.

Energy healing has been around for thousands of years, is considered a complimentary therapy and is being used more in hospitals to treat patients. In fact, several of my Healing Touch trainings have been held at Dupont Hospital for Children in Delaware, where they have a Healing Touch Practitioner on staff to help not only the patients, but their caregivers as well.

Although we are not one hundred percent sure how energy healing works, we believe that energy flows through and around the body in a biofield. Events and illnesses can affect this energy system and flow. Energy healing helps to balance that energy and remove energy that is no longer needed. More research is being done to gain a better understanding of energy healing, and as more people turn to alternative medicine, I believe that this practice will continue to grow.

Energy healing is currently being used to treat a wide variety of issues such as stress, posttraumatic stress disorder (PTSD), side effects of chemotherapy, fibromyalgia, and chronic pain. Energy healing is used to help people as they go through transitions such as divorce and dealing with the loss of a loved one. It is also being used in hospice as people transition from life to death.

I fell in love with energy healing the first time I encountered it. It felt so natural to me that I decided to become skilled in the process. I have seen wonders worked with energy healing and I am glad to see it being used more in Western medicine. I credit energy healing in large part with my own healing process and helping me to reclaim my moxie. I also credit energy healing with keeping my fibromyalgia in check.

I am a hybrid healer, meaning that I incorporate techniques from different modalities into my energy healing practice. One of the most well-known modalities is Reiki, but there are others such as Healing Touch and Therapeutic Touch. And yes, energy work can also be done on animals. I am a Healing Touch for Animals practitioner.

At this point, I feel that it is important to take a moment to talk about healing versus curing. There is a difference between being healed and being cured. You can be healed without being cured and be cured without being healed. It is a widely-held belief that being cured is the removal of symptoms and the elimination of disease. Curing is what most doctors intend to do with their patients. Curing, most often, requires an outside source for the process. Healing, on the other hand, is an independent process and has to do with the wholeness or totality of the patient. Healing can be done using an outside process such as a healer, but it can also be done by the patient. Healing is when everything works in harmony. Healing involves every facet of the individual.

There are many modalities that fall under the umbrella of holistic work such as acupuncture, acupressure, massage therapy, essential oil therapy, and even shamanism, but this list falls short of the extensiveness of this field. Each individual must take his or her own path towards well-being and healing. Don't allow others to dictate your healing process by steering you in a certain direction. Go with what feels right for you. Do your research and don't be afraid to ask lots of questions.

And don't stop there.

Surround yourself with words and voices that reinforce your values. Surround yourself with things that up-lift and support you in your quest to reclaim your moxie. Seek out books that keep you in a positive and motivated state that can provide ways to help you. Thanks to technology, even people who don't like to read, now have the option of listening to audiobooks or even watching videos of motivational speakers on YouTube. The more you surround yourself with positive messages, the easier it becomes to internalize them and help in the healing process. I personally have all of these things at my disposal. It is especially helpful when things get overwhelming or I feel those moxie-diminishing gremlins sneaking in. I just put my earbuds in and listen to one of my favorite authors or motivational recordings to help keep me uplifted and focused on where I need to be. When I find myself stressed, I listen to reiki healing music. This is the way I am able to shut things out and stay focused on keeping that flame burning bright.

Instead of wasting your time on social media, which is draining on a good day, make the decision to only allow positive things in your life that will assist in the development of your mind and spirit. Some of my favorite authors and their books are listed in the reference section at the back of this book. Although I've read many books, the authors who have had a significant impact on my life are Tony

Robbins, Jen Sincero, Tama Kieves, and Will Bowen. Their style speaks to me, but there are many others out there. Find someone who speaks your language.

Go to seminars, workshops, and other events where you can learn new ways to raise your vibrational frequencies. Sometimes just being there, around the energy of other people like you, who also want to raise their frequencies, can help you immensely. Remember, you are not the only one seeking to reclaim your moxie—there are lots of others out there and it's good to be around your own people. Who knows, you might even discover some new friends who wouldn't mind keeping you company as you walk along your journey.

Remember, learning never stops. Not for you, not for me, not for anyone who is seeking personal growth. I personally believe that when you stop growing, you start dying. I don't care how good you feel about your life. It doesn't matter if you are an expert in your field. You need growth. You need development. You need to be ever-reaching for that next level. That is what keeps vibrational frequencies high. That is what keeps moxie fresh and sassy and that's what we're aiming for.

I am constantly attending workshops, lectures and events to add to my personal development repertoire. When I don't attend these functions or stop learning new things, I feel as though I begin to stagnate. I can feel that flame start to dull a wee bit. It's almost like a thirst that constantly needs to be quenched. There is always something new to learn. Sometimes it's new techniques for energy healing and coaching. Sometimes it's just for my own personal growth. Some functions last an hour and others last for days as a full-immersion process.

One of the most exciting things I've done for my own personal development was to attend a Tony Robbins event. Imagine spending four, twelve to fourteen-hour days at an event with over twelve thousand people, just like you, who want great things in life and are seeking personal growth. I don't have to tell you how intense the energy in that arena was. What an incredibly beautiful experience I shared with thousands of people who are just like me. I won't lie. It was a shit-ton of money, but you know what? I would do it all over again in a heartbeat because it was an investment in myself. I learned so much about myself and the things that were limiting growth in several areas of my life. I discovered several new things that were holding me back in my life. I let go of a bunch of crap from my past during those four days and ended up with twelve thousand new friends who continue to stay connected through social media groups. We continue to encourage each other on a daily basis as we achieve our goals. Oh, and I walked across hot coals like a badass and officially became a Firewalker. If you can get to a Tony Robbins event, I highly recommend it.

This chapter has been about healing and how best to help you make it happen. Understand that there is no one-size-fits-all package when it comes to healing. Each healing journey must be custom made-to-order for each individual in order for it to be most effective. Choose what works best for you, and don't worry about what other people think, or if you're being judged. This is your healing. This is your moxie that is being reclaimed. And honestly, part of that moxie is not giving a rat's ass what anybody else thinks. Do what you need to do to heal.

Forgiveness

The subject of forgiveness can be difficult for many people because they somehow feel that it weakens them as individuals. They feel that by forgiving, they have somehow allowed others to have "gotten over" on them. Of all the things we need to do in order to reclaim our moxie, forgiveness may be the toughest one for some people. Boy, we just don't want to give this one up. Let's not forget how many times we've said, "I may forgive, but I'll never forget." So, I'll let you in on a little secret. Forgiving doesn't mean you have to forget. Actually, forgiveness really has very little to do with the other person. It pretty much only has to do with you.

It is really important to understand the next two sentences, so I want you to read them carefully. Forgiveness is not about reconciliation with another person. It is about releasing the resentment and negative energy that are holding you back from fully enjoying your life.

How long have you been walking around holding a grudge against someone because they wronged you in some way?

Yeah, I get it. I've been there myself, and I hear it from clients all the time.

"You have no idea what that person did to me."

Well, I'm here to tell you, that if you don't release that energy, that person will continue to affect and harm you in all aspects of your life. They will continue to harm you physically, emotionally, and spiritually. Just think about how you are responding right now as I even mention the idea of forgiveness towards that person. Are you angry? Indignant? Can you feel your blood pressure climbing? If so, then they still continue to harm you. I know someone who talks about events that happened years ago as if they just happened yesterday. They conjure up the same anger and hatred that they had when the events originally occurred. Their face gets contorted and their voice rises in anger as they go on about how they've been screwed by people.

Really? Do you really want to carry all that anger around with you for the rest of your life?

We've already covered the whole anger thing several chapters ago, so I'm not going to repeat how much harm it is doing to you. By now, you should be getting a handle on it because it's going to put a damper on the entire process of reclaiming your moxie if you don't. But letting go of anger also means finding forgiveness so that you can ultimately release that negative energy from your being.

Listen, I know it's not easy. Growth never is, but in order to grow, you must allow forgiveness to occur. You must decide that whatever someone did to you, it is now in the past and you no longer allow that energy to surround you. You must release it. Trust me, you're going to feel better. You're going to sleep better. You're going to live better.

So, what does forgiveness have to do with moxie, you may be asking? After all, moxie is about tenacity, fearlessness, and guts. Forgiveness seems weak, you might be saying. It seems like your relenting. Why, if I'm reclaiming my moxie, do I have to go all soft and start forgiving people? Well, Grasshopper, I must tell you that reclaiming moxie is a holistic process. You can't pick and choose which areas of your life you fix. You must fix them all. Forgiveness doesn't mean that you go soft and let others walk all over you. It means that you acknowledge something or someone that harmed you and overcome it by releasing it from your own energy. Moxie equals growth in all areas of your life.

Simply, acknowledge that what was done to you was pretty shitty and let it go. Here's the great part about forgiveness—you don't have to even tell the other person that you forgave them. You don't have to have some long heart-to-heart conversation with them. You don't even have to see them in person. You can see them in your mind. As I've said before, hurt people, hurt people. See them as what or who they are—scared, hurt or insecure individuals who do or say not-so-kind things as a way of lashing out. Then let it go.

I speak from experience. I went through a divorce that left me and my children homeless. My ex-husband did not want to make things easy for us. We struggled financially and emotionally. I hated him so much that I wished he would die. When I finally decided to forgive and release the negative energy that surrounded me, something pretty cool happened. I felt as if there was an incredible weight being lifted off me. He could no longer control my feelings and emotions. I felt empowered for the first time in a long time. All the anger I had towards him subsided as I came to the realization that his choices were just that—his choices. I chose to live my life with joy and happiness. I can tell you, it was probably one of the best things I have ever done for myself. Did I speak to him to forgive him? No. I just did it in my mind and so can you. Now, before you start going off on some hate-fest towards ex-spouses, I want to use this story as an example of what happens when people make choices based on fear or anger. Divorce is an extremely difficult process and when people are fearful or angry, they often react in ways that are not in their best interest. Do not make your decisions based on fear or anger because these decisions will never benefit you. Never allow someone to change the person you are. Always be your authentic self.

And for those of you who think that forgiving someone who mistreated you means that you're letting them get away with something, I ask you not to worry about that. They're not getting away with anything. Might I remind you about Madam Karma? Look, she's got this. Let her take care of it.

So here is one of those difficult tasks that I am going to ask of you, and you guessed it, it's about forgiveness. I want you to grab a piece of paper and write a letter to the person or people who are in need of your forgiveness. Write out what they did to you and how it made you feel. Don't be afraid to use the words *hurt* or *angry* in your letter. Be honest. Pour your emotions out onto the paper and don't worry about the grammar and punctuation. Your focus is on the person and the act. Then let them know that you forgive them and are releasing the grip they hold on you. Let them know that instead of holding onto anger and hurt, you choose to hold onto love and joy. Then take that letter and burn it. As it goes up in smoke, so goes your negative feelings of hurt and anger that have held you back all this time. Release them and begin to experience life beyond forgiveness.

If you decide to forgive someone by speaking or writing to them directly, that certainly is another option, but it is not required in order for forgiveness to occur. As I said before, forgiveness is not always about the other person.

And while we're on the subject of forgiveness, my friend, don't forget the most important act of forgiveness, and that is to yourself. After all, no one's been tougher on you than you. It's time to treat yourself with a little more kindness. Forgive yourself for all your imperfections, for all the mistakes you've made in your life, because it's okay to be imperfect and make mistakes. Understand that the beautiful act of forgiving yourself allows you to grow. Forgive yourself for all the people you've hurt, with or without intention because sometimes it's unavoidable even when we try our best to prevent it. Understand that you are human and therefore have succumbed to emotions and lashing out at others, sometimes without merit. If your words or actions have hurt others, then you might want to assess that and ask forgiveness from them.

So, if you've still got that pen and paper out, I want you to write a letter of forgiveness to yourself. You've spent many years being angry at yourself for decisions you've made, things you've allowed to happen, and stuff that you've blamed yourself for. You've been harder on yourself than anyone else in this world, and because of that, you share some responsibility for your moxie being dimmed. Take this opportunity to write that letter, fully forgiving yourself for everything you've done to hurt you and your moxie throughout your life. Get it all written down, burn the letter, and release all the negative energy. *But what if I want to keep the letter, Karen?* Then keep it. You began the process of healing and releasing the energy as you wrote the letter. If you choose to keep it and reread it from time to time as a reminder to forgive yourself, then so be it. Remember, this is *your* healing process.

Forgiving yourself and others is vital to the healing process. I know it can be difficult, but as I've said before, personal growth does not come easy. If you want that moxie to grow and thrive, then you've got to do some really hard work. You've come so far from where you first began in this journey. You've spent so much time getting rid of all the crap you no longer need in your life—all the baggage associated with pain, guilt, fear, and anger. Now you've worked on forgiveness. Don't think all this stuff hasn't had a positive effect on your moxie. It has, even if you're not quite feeling it yet. Don't forget, we have to clear out the old bad stuff in order to make room for the new good stuff. You are doing great!

Stop Trying to Be Perfect...
You're Better Than That

We live in a society that depends a great deal on perfection. We want the perfect job, the perfect house, and the perfect body. We are bombarded with ads that tell us what ideals we must live up to. Use this product to get the perfect hair or perfect skin. Try this product to get down to the perfect weight. How much money and time have we spent in our attempts to achieve this perfection, only to find out that we continually fall short?

We see everyone on social media trying to put forth a perfect smoke-screen of their lives. We only have their written word that things are going so "perfectly" in their lives, but we don't, nor will we ever know for sure, if this is truly the case. Yet, we still compare ourselves. Our cooking isn't as good as theirs. Our kids aren't as smart or well-behaved as theirs. We're not as creative as them. We're not as glamorous as them. They have the perfect marriage. We just don't measure up.

Trying to keep up with the Joneses, and constantly comparing yourself with others on social media, will result in a serious ass-beating of your moxie because it wreaks havoc on your confidence. You begin to wonder what is wrong with you. Why can't your life be as perfect as theirs? Why can't you seem as happy? The next thing you know, you're sitting there all depressed and deflated, and that beautiful flame starts to dull. That's because you are constantly trying to achieve everyone else's ideals of perfection and not your own. Do not allow this to happen. You don't deserve this and neither does your moxie.

Perfection, or the ideal vision of it, is brought to us courtesy of our society. It's been this way for a long time. We hold ourselves up to images that we may never be able to achieve and goals that we may never be able to accomplish. But why? Why are we so afraid to just be us? Why do we torment ourselves by trying to be someone, or something, we're not? If you are looking to reclaim that moxie, then you are going to have to abandon this way of thinking because it doesn't serve you or benefit you in any way.

When I decided to run for local office, I was not yet thirty years old. At that time, my hair was long, I wore the type of clothes most people in their twenties would wear, and it was not unusual for me to wear makeup. I remember knocking on doors in my community to ask for votes and the first thing people would ask is how old I was. I didn't fit their ideal of what a local councilwoman would look like. I was too young and not conservative enough for them. To get over their preconception of how I should look, I began to wear my hair in a bun and started wearing less makeup. That seemed to be more acceptable to voters. Even after I won my election, I still felt as though I had to dress a certain way, look a certain way, and speak a certain way. Eventually, not being me began to wear on, well…me. I didn't feel authentic. I felt like I was trying to please others, instead of being my own true self. I began to realize that my constituents didn't need someone who fit into a certain mold, they needed someone who would do an excellent job. My uniqueness deserved to be celebrated. From then on, I started acting, speaking, and dressing in a way that suited me, not others. Did some people have an issue with it? Yeah, but I didn't care, because I stayed true to who I was and remained focused on doing important things for my community. Most people got over it. Screw those who didn't. When we live our lives trying to be something we're not, we do ourselves, and our moxie, a big disservice.

Ok, I said in the beginning of this book that I would ask some difficult things of you and I meant it. I know the forgiveness thing really stuck in your craw, but this one might get the book thrown in the trash. I'm going to ask you to stop spending so much time on social media. Just stay off it for a while because comparing your life to that of others ends up beating the crap out of your moxie. Stop looking to see what others are doing with their lives and start focusing on making yours better. Take a break from it for a month and I can guarantee that you will begin to feel much better about yourself. It is time wasting and confidence stifling. I am also going to ask you to turn your back on the ideals that society places on us. Stop worrying about how others look and live, because they are not you. Here's what else I ask—that you be the truest, most awesome authentic self that only you know how to be because that is who you are. Just be you, simply because no one else can.

I've got a newsflash for you...

While you've been running around trying to be the perfect someone else, you've been missing out on being the truly perfect YOU. You see there is none other like you. You are the most perfect you that there is. You are unique in so many ways that it defies the imagination, and yet you've been beating yourself up because you keep trying to be the perfect someone else. And that's just silly, because it won't work.

Let's just think about sunsets for a moment. They all look perfect, each and every one of them, but just as every sunset is unique, so are you. If we were to view sunsets as we view ourselves, we probably wouldn't be so kind to them.

Ugh, just look at those clouds! They are nowhere near as fluffy as the ones we saw yesterday. Sure, there's gold and orange colors in the sky today, but where's the pink and purple that was there last week? Hmm, the sky could even be a little brighter. There's not enough of this. There's not enough of that.

We could make anything look imperfect it we try hard enough. Well, it's time to stop all this talk about perfection based on the ideals of others. Perfection isn't natural—it's man made. Nothing in nature is perfect. It's unique. It's beautiful. But perfect? No. If that were the case, every snowflake would be the same. Every tree would have the same number of branches and leaves. Every waterfall would look just like the next. And every sunset would look the same exact way every night. Everything natural would be...boring.

And, so would you.

Stand out. Embrace your uniqueness. That is what gives you your beauty. That is what makes you nothing at all like the rest of us. You're not a creature made by man. You're a creature made by something so much better. Be that bright and unique being that you were meant to be. Stop trying to be everyone else's vision of perfect. You're so much better than that. Let that moxie shine through in whatever authentic way it wants. Dress in whatever fashion suits you. Laugh however loud and boisterous as you want. Sing out of tune and dance like you just don't care. Don't allow others to dictate their ideals onto you. Think about who the real you is and just go with it. And don't be afraid of what others might say or think. Aren't you tired of being boxed-in? Aren't you tired of having to conform to the mold of others?

Okay, get out that journal. Let's start rediscovering the real you—the authentic you—the you that only you can do. I want you to write down ten things that you are good at. If you are struggling to come up with something, then imagine yourself as a friend writing down what you're good at. Maybe you're good at talking to people or maybe you're an awesome cook. I want to see some bragging here, people! And don't tell me that you're not good at anything—every one of us is good at something. That is how we discover our purpose, so stop feeling sorry for yourself and start writing. Next, I want you to write down ten unique things about you. Maybe you've got some cute freckles across the bridge of your nose or maybe you've got a couple of crooked toes. What sets you apart from others?

In case you haven't realized it, you are a spectacular, one-of-a-kind ball of awesomeness. Embrace it all—the things you rock and the things that make you special. Your moxie cannot be contained, so stop squelching it just to please others and fit into their version of perfection. Just be the perfect you, the one who can't be defined by anyone else on this planet. Unleash your uniquely badass self and allow that moxie to light up this world.

Shine, baby, shine!

Gratitude makes for a Great Attitude

*C*ount your blessings. No, really. Count your blessings.

If there's one thing that can change your life and bring in more abundance, it's the mindset of gratitude. I cannot stress enough the importance of gratitude in your life and how much of an impact it will have on your moxie. Gratitude is more than just an action; it creates a shift in your mindset, changes the way you think about things, and provides you with a better outlook in your life. When life doesn't seem to be going so well, the simple act of gratitude can be a real game changer for many people. It's really hard to be in a crappy mood, and hating everything around you, when you have a mindset of gratitude.

I always suggest that my clients start a journal to record ten things that they are grateful for every day. It's pretty easy the first day, but once you go through your family, friends and pets, things start to become a bit more challenging. This is where you have to dig a little deeper to find the "not so in your face" things to be grateful for. How about a sunrise or sunset? Maybe your vision, hearing, and the ability to walk? How about that television you watch the news on every night? It's funny how we tend to look for the really big things to be grateful for when there are really so many little things in our life that we take for granted.

I remember opening up my fridge one morning and having some stuff fall out and hit me on the foot as it tumbled to the floor. Although my immediate reaction was to complain about how much stuff there was on the shelves, and that we couldn't possibly cram another thing into the damn fridge, I quickly bit my tongue. Instead, I stood there silently and became grateful for having an abundance of food, because there are many people who open the door of their fridge every day in this country to see empty shelves. Hell, there are many people in this world who have no idea what a refrigerator even is. And I'm about to bitch because I've got too much food?

Let's think about this. By not showing gratitude it is essentially a slap in the face to your creator, whether it's God, Universal Energy, or whatever you want to call that which has provided you with all that you have. It's like a spoiled, ungrateful child showing no appreciation for what they have, but wanting more.

Really?

Having gratitude for all the good things in life is a piece of cake. Of course, we're happy for all the good things in life, who wouldn't be? But how about the not-so-good things in life? Sometimes it's not so obvious. Well, that's where we start to separate the children from the adults, my friend. Finding gratitude in things not-so-great is where you truly start to experience some personal and spiritual growth, and that is when your moxie grows.

Try to find gratitude in all things, even things that are not-so-good. My good friend, Steve, had a full-time sales job but sold real estate part time. I can remember him calling me one day and telling me how upset he was because he was just laid off from his full-time job. I told him that things happen for a reason and to be grateful that they laid him off. I said that this might be the best thing that could have happened to him because now he could devote himself to selling real estate full-time. You know what? He's been kicking real estate ass ever since!

So, what are some other bad things to be grateful for? How about being grateful for finding out your boyfriend or girlfriend was a jerk and you only had to spend five years with them instead of ten. Or that an illness brought your family closer together and gave you a deeper appreciation of life. There is always something to be grateful for. Someone once asked me, "Well, should I be grateful for cancer?" I told them, "No, you don't have to be grateful for cancer, but be grateful for being surrounded by a supportive family, medical insurance to cover a good portion of your bills, and dedicated doctors, nurses and scientists who are trying to find ways to make you well."

Does being grateful mean that you need to be happy all the time? Absolutely not. Don't equate gratitude with happiness. You are entitled to times of sadness throughout your life, but during those times you can still find gratitude for things in your life. Sometimes the only thing that can help you get through those difficult times is having a sense of gratitude. And don't assume that someone who makes gratitude an important part of their lives is someone who has had an easy life. I've had people tell me, "Oh, sure, it's easy for you to be grateful, you haven't had the life I did." I tell them, "You don't know me, and you don't know what I've been through, so don't assume it's all been good." I'm pretty sure we've all gone through rough times in our lives. The difference is that some of us choose to focus on the things we have to be grateful for instead of the things we have to complain about. I recently spoke with someone about how people assume a life of gratitude equates to a life of happiness. She confided that her son was murdered and that she, too, encountered people who made that assumption. She said that it was not until she began focusing on gratitude, that she began to heal from that tragedy.

Moxie loves gratitude and gratitude brings abundance. Although I've discussed the law of attraction several chapters ago, I think this is a good time to reiterate how much a positive attitude and the simple act of gratitude can have an incredible impact on your life. When you are grateful, you raise your vibrational frequency. The things you desire at higher frequencies are attracted to you. You will find that abundance flows, and your moxie grows. You become a super-charged moxie magnet. So, start kissing the days of bitterness and complaining away—they're not doing you any good anyway. Make gratitude your new best friend and I guarantee that you will begin to see life in a whole new light.

No slacking on this one, my friend. Get that journal started today. Write your list of ten things that you're grateful for each day and I promise that you will see a difference in every area of your life. As the days go on, and you become consciously aware of how much you really have to be grateful for, you will begin to see a shift in your mindset. You will experience more joy, more peace and more abundance.

After all, how can you expect to receive more in your life if you aren't grateful for what you already have?

Thank Your Sacred Clown

One of my favorite authors is Will Bowen, who wrote A Complaint Free World. If you haven't read his books or checked out his YouTube videos, then I encourage you to do so. He's got a great way of connecting with people and his stories have tremendous meaning. I remember listening to one of Will's stories about the sacred clown which is part of the Native American culture. The sacred clown is a contrarian member of the tribe. That means that their job is to essentially do, react, and speak the opposite of the people around them in order to get them riled up as much as possible. They purposely try to irritate and upset people. The more they get under the skin of others, the better they are doing their job. I'll bet, at this very moment, you've come up with at least one sacred clown in your own life. Oh, you know who I'm talking about. It's that person who drives you bat-shit crazy. Their very existence makes you let out long dramatic sighs of frustration and seething. We all have these sacred clowns in our lives, and if we let them, they will challenge every ounce of our being.

Ah, but that's the true role of the sacred clown. To challenge every ounce of our being and help us grow as a person. How many times did you do or accomplish something with that *I'll show you* or *you're not stopping me* attitude because of something someone either said or did? Sacred clowns are put in our lives to challenge us and provide obstacles to keep us from doing things. Our job is to find ways around these challenges, move beyond them, and accomplish what we set out to do. They need to make us miserable, because that's when we almost always take action.

I had a friend who always talked about moving to Florida. She loved the warm weather and visited the state whenever she could. I often told her that she should move, but I think there was a part of her that was scared to just take the leap to up and relocate. Things were going well for her. She was very happy in her job and thought she would continue doing that job for many years, but still she talked about one day moving down to the Sunshine State with its turquoise waters and sandy beaches. She resigned herself to thinking that a move to Florida would just have to wait until she retired. Then, she got transferred to a new group and began working for the biggest jerk ever. He made her life completely miserable. She loved her work as a scientist and thought she would retire as one, but because of her jerk boss, she did something she never thought she'd do in a million years— she actually started looking for other jobs within the company. So, when a sales position came up in Florida, she quickly applied—and you guessed it—got the job. She was also told that she would receive a nice increase in salary, sales bonuses, the company would pay her moving expenses, and even handle the sale of her house. She was over-the-moon happy. Upon accepting the job, she went back to that jerk boss of hers and actually thanked him. She told him that he was the worst boss she ever had, and if he hadn't treated her so badly, she would have never looked for a new opportunity, which in the end, was a better job than she could have imagined. Oh, and it placed her ass in sunny Florida, thereby fulfilling a dream. That boss was one of her sacred clowns in this life. Because of him she did something she never thought she would do. She went outside her comfort zone and sought out a new opportunity, where she ended up with a better life.

I like to think that sacred clowns are sometimes put in our lives to motivate us to do the things we might never have done on our own. They are responsible for helping us reclaim our moxie because they help us recognize that we are fighters and can accomplish anything we set our minds to do. Sometimes they are put in our lives to help us find a better path. I've had many sacred clowns in my life who thought they were hurting me by their childish and mean actions. They thought their roadblocks would be enough to stop me from gaining more in life and becoming a better person, but it only drove me to figure out ways to overcome those challenges. Because of my sacred clowns, I have accomplished things that I would have never even dreamed of. I ended up on much better paths than I ever would have if they hadn't come into my life. I now know that there is nothing that I can't do. I am unstoppable. And so are you.

It's journal time, my friend. I want you to stop for a moment and think about the sacred clowns who have come into your life. What have you learned from them? Don't tell me you haven't learned anything, because I know you have. You just have to stop being so pissed for a moment and dig deeper to figure it out. Maybe you learned to be more patient. Maybe you learned how to do something that you didn't think was possible. Maybe you learned that you had more moxie and stamina than you originally thought. Sacred clowns are placed in our lives to help us, whether we believe it or not. They provide us with a benefit, so we just need to figure out what it is.

So, if you have that one person who tends to get under your skin, and pretty much pushes you to the edge of insanity, they could very well be your sacred clown. It would be easy to hate them, but don't. Think of them as a test or a challenge that you need to overcome. They may even be guiding you towards a better life. Thank them for making you a better person. Oh, and don't forget to send a big old energy hug their way, because more than anyone else, they really need it.

Self-Care

What is self-care? I like to say it's the belief in your value or self-worth. It's the act of doing something special for yourself in an effort to show that you are worthy of such actions. In plain words, it's pampering or spoiling yourself. It's making yourself number one, even if it's only for a little while.

Now, for those of you who are going to give me that "isn't that selfish?" shit, I'm here to officially let you know that it's okay to be selfish. In fact, I often require it of my clients as part of my coaching. Being selfish does not mean "it's all about me, just me, and only me." Being selfish is recognizing your own value and treating yourself as you would treat someone else with the same value. Being selfish means that it is absolutely okay to be good to you. I have learned over many years, that if you don't recognize your own value, no one else will either. If you've been complaining about everybody treating you like a doormat, then maybe it's because you're sending out the energy of a doormat. You cannot reclaim your moxie if you're running yourself ragged and not taking care of you.

There is a reason why they tell the adults on an aircraft to put the oxygen masks on themselves before they attempt to place them on children. That is because precious time needs to be placed on taking care of yourself so that you can then take care of others. Listen up caretakers. This self-care thing is especially written for you. We cannot possibly operate at our best when we constantly place others first and place ourselves last. That my love, is how the whole martyr syndrome starts.

We all know the martyr. They walk around life telling everyone about how much they sacrifice for others and how they put themselves last.

"I never have any time for myself."

"I spend all my money on everyone else and never have any left for me."

"Don't worry about me; as long as everyone else is happy."

"Go ahead, everyone, have a seat at the table. I'll just stand by the island and eat."

Ugh! I can actually hear Eeyore the donkey in my head. Please don't get caught up in this nonsense. Being the martyr only leads to resentment, which in turn, leads to you really being pissed off because after you've given everything to everyone, there's nothing left for you. You'll quietly seethe at the fact that you're being sucked dry and you'll secretly blame others, when it's you who are actually causing the problem for yourself. I've always said that some people need to be needed. That is just how they define themselves. I've never quite understood that mentality; maybe it has something to do with control. If they are the one that everyone runs to, they feel valued. A lot of moms are guilty of this behavior. If you are one of those moms, stop. You're doing everyone, including yourself a big disservice. Yeah, it's great to have people need you, but eventually you are going to need yourself and there will be nothing left of you—for you—but a pathetic, empty shell. Cut the cord, insist on some independence for you and them, and start focusing on taking care of yourself. Personally, I never really got into that whole "being needed" mentality. I always took the opposite approach with my kids. I wanted them to be independent, and be able to get along without me, because one day they will have to. I am here as a resource if my kids can't figure something out on their own or with the help of each other.

So, here's some seriously good advice. Stop being the martyr. Get over yourself. I know it's hard to believe, but everyone will survive without you throwing yourself on the stake for them. Being the martyr never ends well. If you don't believe me, then just check out some history books.

Trust me, I've been there. Raising four kids took its toll because I constantly put their needs above mine. That's not to say that I don't love my children—I love them with all my heart, but I found that I couldn't be an effective parent when I'd given my all and there was nothing left for me. When I started doing little things for me, I started becoming a more relaxed, happier parent who could devote more time and energy to my kids. This is a tough thing to wrap your head around, especially if you're a mom. We give up so much for our kids. We would give them the last crumb in the fridge if we had to. But that's the thing—we don't usually end up in a situation where we have to give up the last of anything for our kids. We don't normally have to give up our lives for them, so we need to stop acting like we do. Everything we do for our kids, or anyone else for that matter, does not have to be some form of self-sacrifice. We are entitled to good things as much as everyone else. We are entitled to quiet time and pampering. We are entitled to all the little guilty pleasures that this life has to offer. I remember the first time, in like forever, that I bought myself a pair of really expensive sneakers. You know, not the kind I usually bought that would fall apart after being worn for two months. One of my kids looked at them and said, "They look expensive," and I said, "Yep, they were, but they didn't quite add up to all the money I've spent on sneakers for you guys over the years. In fact, when I look at it that way, I kind of think they were a bargain."

So how do you invoke self-care? Well, the first step is to acknowledge that you have needs and are worthy of that self-care. That means that you're going to have to start treating yourself a little bit better. You know, like you would treat someone else who wasn't you. You might be resistant to this whole self-care thing, but believe me, once you get acclimated to it, you're gonna want to be my new best friend for pushing you into this.

Start off by buying or doing something you've been putting off. Take a yoga class. Make time each evening to read. Yes, it's ok to treat yourself to something. You fully have my permission, but more importantly, give yourself permission. In order to reclaim your moxie, you need to really begin to understand your own value and self-worth. Self-care means that you need to be focusing on what makes you whole. This includes your mental, emotional, spiritual, and physical well-being. Everything has to be in balance for moxie to grow and thrive. If one of these things is off balance, then you need to address it and get it back to its rightful place.

Repeat after me. "I am worthy of good things. It's okay for me to treat myself well. The world won't end, and my children won't starve, if I treat myself to something nice."

So, here's what I want you to do. Start making a list of things you've been putting off doing or buying for yourself. The list can consist of big things, little things, or a combination of both. This is your list—choose whatever you want. Vacations. Massages. A new wardrobe. Write down whatever you consider a treat, guilty pleasure, or something that you've been putting off. Then, don't just sit there and wistfully look at the list—start acting on it. Trust me, when you are feeling good, everyone around you will start feeling the same. You'll have more energy and you won't resent giving some of yourself to help others. Be sure to hang that list where you can see it every day as a reminder to treat yourself to good things in life. You are so worthy of all the good things this life has to offer. It's time that you started recognizing that. If you are in the process of reclaiming that moxie, then you need to understand that you can have wonderful things without feeling guilty. You are entitled to joy and pleasure. Don't deny yourself these things. Your moxie will thank you.

The Power of No

*R*eclaiming your moxie is all about setting boundaries and limitations with people. You need to decide what you will or will not put up with. This is a real challenge for many people and one that you will have to overcome if you really want to reclaim that moxie.

We tend to be people pleasers. We love to make people happy, but sometimes that comes at our own expense. It also means that we have a big issue with the word *no*. We really struggle with this word. It gets to the point where we end up being worn out and exhausted because we do everything people ask of us instead of simply saying *no*. For some reason, we feel as if saying *no* goes against our very being. It's easy to get caught up in the act of saying *yes* and it starts to become a habit without even realizing it. Next thing you know, you're saying *yes* to everything that is being asked of you, even the things you really don't want to do, and it's like you've somehow unlearned

how to say *no*. It ends up with you complaining about how everyone treats you like a doormat.

But reclaiming your moxie is all about finding and being your true self, and your true self is surely not a doormat. When you reclaim your moxie, your life starts taking on a different meaning. It's no longer about doing things that other people want or what's good for them. It's about doing the things that you want and what's good for you. Saying *no* to things you don't want to do equates to saying *yes* to a better, and more stress-free life. When you continually do things that you don't want to do it leads to resentment on multiple levels. You resent the person for asking and you resent yourself for not saying *no*. It's all about control and who you're giving it to. When you learn to embrace that scary word, *no*, you start taking back control of your time, your emotions, and your life. And really, don't you deserve that?

Saying *no* is one of those things that is so difficult to do in the beginning, but trust me, you will find that it really gets easier as you say it more and more. The first few times your tongue may feel swollen, you might wince and say it half-heartedly, you might even whine while you're saying it, as if you're in some sort of pain. Your brain is going to start to tell you all these untruths about how mean and selfish you are. You're going to feel like a jerk. You're going to be sure that everyone thinks you're a total asshole. Just ignore that brain because it's all in your head. Uh, no pun intended.

Saying *no* is going to be hard at first—there is no doubt about it, but you know what? When you finally get up the gumption to say it, you're going to feel as though a tremendous weight has been lifted off your shoulders. You're going to be able to exhale. You're going to feel empowered, and empowerment brings back moxie.

So how do you get your *no* groove going? I suggest you practice saying the word *no* over and over again until it flows easily from your mouth. If you have to sit your ass down in front of a mirror and say it to see what it will look like coming out of your mouth, then even better. Still not sure how to say it? Here are some ideas.

No.

No thank you.

I'm sorry, but no.

I'd love to, but I can't.

I'd really love to, but I can't.

It's nothing personal, it's just a business decision.

I've got way too much on my plate right now.

No. Learn it. Love it. Embrace it. Internalize it as if your moxie depends on it, because it pretty much does.

I know, we all have that fear of what people will think or how they will feel about us if we tell them *no.* They may not call us as much. They may not talk to us as much. They might think we're not so nice. But most of those fears are in our heads. We always fear the worst imaginable thing. Remember, we already discussed fear and decided that we're not going to be scaredy cats anymore. If the consequences of telling people *no* are starting to make your palms sweat and give you anxiety, then you might want to go back and revisit the chapter that talks about scaredy cats. I'm going to let you in on a secret. Telling people *no* is not the end of the world. The majority of people are totally okay with hearing the word *no*. In fact, they will probably tell you that they completely understand. It's not that big of a deal. It's a bigger deal to us in our minds. So, get out of your head.

But, let's say that you are right, and all those things do happen. They don't call you as much. They don't talk to you as much. They don't think you're so nice. So, what's the downside? In my opinion, there is none, but I am seeing somewhat of an upside, like maybe they'll stop asking you to do things that you would rather not do. Maybe they'll respect your time a little more. Maybe they will only come to you when they really need your help, not when they are looking to take advantage of your kindness. What if they *really* get pissed and never want to see you again? Well, I'm thinking that maybe, just maybe, these people shouldn't be in your life anyway.

No is a very liberating word. It frees us from obligations that we never wanted in the first place. It empowers us to do only the things that make us feel worthy and valued. It allows us to set boundaries with those who have a habit of taking advantage of us.

The next time someone asks you to do something you don't want to do, think about it. Think really hard about it and determine how you will feel if you say *yes*. Bitter? Angry? If that is the outcome, then you're pleasing others instead of yourself. You're not speaking your truth and aren't you tired of not speaking your truth?

Trust me, the first *no* is the most difficult one. The more you say it, the easier it gets, the more respect you will feel for yourself, and the more confident you will be with your decisions.

The more you say it, the more moxie grows.

One simple syllable. One powerful word. *No*.

Find Your Voice

When we lose our moxie, we often lose our voice. Past events and relationships stifle us from speaking up and speaking out about things. I remember being told as a child, when I would come home and be proud of something I did, that "self-praise stinks." Hearing those stinging words knocked down my confidence and made it difficult for me to feel good about myself or anything I did. I learned to be silent about my accomplishments and not talk about myself in a good way. It was better to be silent or self-deprecating than it was to be proud of myself. As I grew up that beautiful internal flame became more and more dimmed. When I think back to stuff like that I cringe. I can't imagine telling my children that they aren't special or great, each in their own way, nor can I imagine making fun of the way they look, the way they feel, or the way they think. I can remember when my daughter Katie, who was around seven at the time, announced at the dinner table that she was going to make so much money that they would have to make up a new number to count it all. I looked over at her and said, "Yes you are, girlfriend!" Why would I tell her that what she wanted was not possible? Why would I dim her light? There are enough people in this world that will do that—it's not going to happen with me. I have always encouraged my kids to find their voice—to speak up and be heard. I want them to have all the confidence they deserve so that they can achieve great things in this life. Alright, so now I end up with a bunch of loudmouth kids who take every opportunity to disagree with me, or let me know when I'm wrong, but they have their voice and I wouldn't have it any other way.

Finding your voice is not always about being vocal. It also has to do with your actions, or should I say, inaction. Putting up with things that you don't want, or just allowing things to happen, is a sign that you've lost your voice. Maybe you've become compliant with whatever rules were thrown at you and you didn't want to "rock the boat." Maybe you've lost your ability to fight for what you believe is right. Maybe you've even lost the ability to fight for yourself. But just because it's been like that doesn't mean that it has to stay like that.

When you reclaim your moxie, you begin to once again find your voice. You make the decision that you're going to step out of your comfort zone and do things differently. You begin to realize that you've spent enough time taking crap throughout your life and it's gotten you absolutely nowhere. Your silence has become deafening and unbearable. You are frustrated and angry. You may even blame yourself for the loss of your voice. It gets to a point where you cannot stand another minute of having your voice silenced. This is the turning point for you. This is the point where you feel as though you need to be heard. You're ready to abandon the silence and scream from the mountain top, *I am not going to take this shit for one more second. I will never be silenced again!* That's the moment you're ready to put on your moxie armor and head into battle.

I went through a bad divorce (I'm not sure there are too many good ones) which had me in courtrooms more times than I ever cared to think about. Divorce is bad enough, but when you spend so much time in court, you end up incredibly beaten down. I had enough stress of taking care of four kids without constantly spending my time in a courtroom. While some people feel the need to do battle, I am someone who prefers to just go along my merry way in an effort to move forward with my life. I remember just wanting the whole thing to stop, so that I could live my life in peace and place my focus on the important things, such as finding us a place to live, making enough money to feed everyone, and trying to heal. It got to the point where I didn't even care about the outcome of the court cases and I just wanted it to be over. I would take whatever was thrown at me because I didn't have any fight left in me. I felt as if my strength was totally depleted and my voice was gone.

Going to court so many times really took its toll on my psyche and my moxie. I suffered PTSD from it all. I would cringe at the thought of walking up the steps of a courthouse—any courthouse—and it didn't matter what the circumstances were. Just going to the courthouse to get a passport for my daughter, stopping by the voter registration office, or even paying a stupid tax bill was enough to put me into a nervous sweat. I lived that way for many years, and those feelings became a new normal for me. It's amazing how we adjust ourselves downward and lower our standards to a new normal, when we should really be adjusting ourselves upward and raising our standards. We accept all that is dumped onto us as long as we allow it. And for the longest time, that's how it was for me.

But that was before I reclaimed my moxie.

So, imagine that I'm driving through a little town one day with my husband, and yeah, I might (I say might) have been going a bit over the speed limit, when he gently points out that I just passed a police car sitting in an empty lot. Well, it wasn't long before I began to see some flashing red and blue lights behind me. I pulled over, spoke to the officer, thanked him for his service, and ended up with a speeding ticket. *Can you believe it?* Even after I told him that I'd never gotten a ticket in all my years of driving, he still wrote me one. Sure, he was nice enough and very respectful, but he was young enough to be my son. *Come on, would he write a ticket for his own mom?* I looked down at the ticket and grumbled to my husband that the officer didn't even get my full name right on the damn thing. I think I spent the rest of the day totally flabbergasted that someone would even write me a ticket after all these years. Apparently, the cute smile isn't what it used to be.

One of my good friends, Ray who is a retired police officer, says that he always advises people to just go ahead and fight a ticket by appearing in court, but fighting things hadn't been in my nature when it came to court. I had pretty much decided that I would just pay the ticket. After all, who wants to take a day off of work and drive two hours to spend all day in court? But it was more than that. It meant that I would have to enter a courtroom and speak up to some authority sitting behind a bench. Thoughts of past courtroom experiences came rushing through my head and it scared me. It scared me a lot. I was torn between fighting the ticket, which would result in a major hit on my car insurance—not to mention my wallet, and just going about my life without confrontation or speaking up for myself.

The grace period for paying the ticket was approaching, and I had put off paying that ticket for as long as I could. On the day of reckoning, I went online and was getting ready to just pay it and take my lumps, but something stopped me. I'm not even sure how to explain it. I started looking at the paper the officer gave me with instructions on what I had to do if I wanted to contest it. The ticket was steep at $154, but that is not what was driving me to rethink paying it. I thought about all the years I had gone without getting a ticket (ok, so maybe I got a warning or two), but I had a perfect record. And I was a good driver. But there was something else deep inside of me. Something that said I needed to step up to this fear of court and face it head-on. The worst thing that could happen is that I would be found guilty and have to pay the fine. It seemed as if all my mindfulness training started to come into play as I stopped feeling the fear and started to re-examine the reality of the situation. Not the fear that had been running through my head, but the reality of it all. *The absolute worst that could happen is that I would have to pay the fucking fine.* That's it. Nothing more. The same fine I would have paid online if I chose not to fight the ticket. I had nothing to lose. Absolutely nothing to lose at all.

But I had so much to gain, and it had nothing to do with being found not guilty and saving $154. I would gain so much more than that. I would, once again, find my voice.

And so, it was decided. It was like that moxie flame shot up inside me. I'm not taking this bullshit anymore. I'm going to find my voice. I'm going to face my fear of the courts, march in there, and contest the ticket. Once again, I reminded myself that the worst that could happen, is that I would still have to pay the damn ticket, but I wasn't going to do it without a fight.

So there I was on that day of my hearing, just waiting to be heard. I had proudly printed out my perfect lifetime driving record the day before, so that I would be ready to state my case. I had to fill out some paperwork while I waited. Oh, and I made sure that I corrected my name on the damn form since I was all about speaking my voice that day.

A lieutenant called me into the office to discuss the case.

"You threw me for a loop with your new name," he said.

"That's not a new name, sir. That's my name. I've had it for eight years now."

"Did you just change it on your license?"

"No."

"Well sometimes the computer spits it out in different order."

"No," I told him. "This is the way the officer wrote it on the ticket."

"Do you have the original ticket?" he asked.

"Of course," I said while handing him the ticket. I was feeling pretty smug that morning because I had everything printed out and prepared in a nice folder. I also pulled out my perfect lifetime driving record.

After a few moments of looking over the paperwork in front of him, the lieutenant looked back up at me.

"I'm assuming that's your driving record?"

"Yes, it is. I wanted to show you that I have never gotten a ticket," I said.

"Well, ma'am, I'll do you one better. I'm asking that this case be dismissed because the officer did not put your name correctly on the ticket. We strive for accuracy in this department and we didn't have it this time. You're free to go."

Ok, so I can't tell you how I felt at that moment. It was somewhere between total badass and moxie goddess. I did not have any expectations that day other than I was going to do several things: face my fear of the courts, take a risk and get out of my comfort zone, and find my voice and speak up. The officer wrote my name incorrectly, but it really didn't matter, because the old me would have just paid the ticket. The old me would have just accepted it.

But this wasn't the old me. It was the new me. It was the new me with moxie.

So, here's my advice to you, my love. Take a chance. Take a risk. Don't take crap from anyone. Find that awesome voice that has been sitting there quietly inside you for so long. Open your mouth and let it come out. Find your voice. It's a beautiful voice and it's been quiet for way too long. Start using that word *No* that you learned about in the previous chapter.

Speak up. Speak out. Let that voice be heard.

Start Telling Yourself a Better Story

*O*nce upon a time I mowed the grass.

A lot.

In fact, I mowed the grass every time it needed to be mowed. Did I like mowing the grass all the time? According to my story, yes. It was good for my health. It was great exercise. Even when I was nine months pregnant in the heat of August, and my neighbors asked why my husband wasn't mowing the grass, I told them the same bullshit story that I told myself all those years. It was good for my health. It was great exercise.

I told myself and my neighbors that story so much that I actually started to believe it.

See, that's what happens when you begin to accept standards lower than what you deserve. That's what happens when you don't want to be honest with yourself, let alone with anyone else. You begin to tell yourself a story. If you tell yourself the story often enough, or long enough, you'll begin to believe it.

But you kind of don't.

There's still that voice, also known as moxie, way down deep inside of you, telling you that the story is complete and utter bullshit. It tells you that you deserve better. It tells you that you need to stop putting up with the nonsense, and above all, stop lying to yourself. You end up getting really annoyed at that voice, because you know it's right, but you continue to tell your story.

Let's take a deeper look at this story that I told myself and how it began. The grass would often get high, and asking my husband to help cut it, just didn't seem to be—cutting it. It was one of those things that he kept putting off. So, as to not have my neighbors talking about the ratty house on the block with the tall grass, I would just go ahead and do it. It eventually got to the point where, if I wanted to continue to have a lawn that would not get me cited by the local government, I would mow the grass. Why didn't I just yell and scream at my husband to mow the grass? Good question. Mainly because it seemed to do no good. We didn't have the same values or priorities. Instead of constantly complaining, I just found it easier, and less confrontational, to do it myself. He never stepped up and so it fell completely on me. Did I resent doing it? Absolutely. But I did it and continued to do it. After a while I became more complacent. If the job was going to get done, it would be me doing it. When neighbors questioned me, I didn't want to feel like an ass and say that my husband was too uncaring to do it, so I made up some bullshit story about it being good exercise. Yeah, because every pregnant woman about to give birth in August wants to get some extra exercise mowing the fucking grass. But that's the story I told my neighbors and myself to cope with a crappy situation. So, when did I stop mowing the grass? When I filed for divorce.

We tell ourselves lots of stories throughout our lives. Maybe you're telling yourself one right now. Like that you're okay with being in a relationship with someone who is not right for you, or doesn't treat you well, but you continue staying because they're really "not that bad." After all, they could be worse. Oh, he's still a jerk, but not as big a jerk as the one you *could* have. Are you in a toxic relationship with a parent or sibling and telling yourself that being treated badly is okay because they're the only family you have? Or maybe you continue going to work at a job where you're not valued and treated poorly, because it's paying the bills and you probably couldn't get a higher paying job somewhere else. Maybe you're telling yourself that you'll deal with the current situation, whatever it may be, because there's nothing better in your future.

I know someone whose cars are constantly breaking down. He brushes it off and says he likes to work on cars, but I have to wonder, does he really like working on cars, just to be able to drive them, or is that a story he began telling himself because at some point in his life he couldn't afford a dependable car?

You see, we tell ourselves these stories in an effort to save ourselves from feeling bad about the hard truth. But it's all bullshit. We are actually telling ourselves a lie so that we are not confronted with the truth, because if we were really truthful with ourselves, we'd be embarrassed or ashamed that we allowed our standards to sink below what we really deserve. But here's the problem. We may be able to fool our brain into believing the story, but our moxie will always call bullshit on it, because it knows better. Our moxie knows that we're settling for less than we deserve. It knows that we've lowered our standards. It screams at us to stop lying to ourselves and do something about it. But we don't listen to our moxie. We continue to tell the story and essentially tell our moxie to be quiet.

Who's dimming our moxie now?

Here's the thing. We know that moxie has external enemies. They are the people who seek to make us feel less than we truly are. We encounter them all throughout our lives. But moxie also has internal enemies. They come in the form of doubt, procrastination, indecision, and deceiving ourselves. These internal enemies actually have the power to hurt us more than the external ones, because they are the ones we can't get away from by walking away, hanging up our phones, or turning off social media. They are the ones that insidiously creep into our brains, silence our voice, and eventually harm our moxie. If we're going to eliminate the external enemies in our lives, then we're also going to have to eliminate the internal ones as well.

So what story have you been telling yourself? That you're good with whatever you're dealing with? That it will eventually work itself out? That this lower standard is acceptable?

Stop telling yourself the story that you don't deserve more than what you have.

Stop telling yourself that you are destined to be mediocre.

And for God's sake, stop lying to your moxie. There's been enough damage done to it by the external enemies, let's get a handle on those internal ones as well. Reclaiming your moxie is all about speaking your truth. Let's start doing that today.

Start telling yourself a different story—a better story. Like maybe you're smart enough or qualified enough to get that job that you really want instead of that crappy job you're currently dealing with. Or that relationships can be great, and you deserve to be with someone who treats you with kindness and respect. Maybe it's time to tell yourself that you are unstoppable—that all the crap you've gone through in life has prepared you for whatever obstacles you'll face in the future. It's time to tell yourself the truth—that you can do or have anything you want in this life. That you are entitled to incredible joy and happiness. That you deserve someone in your life who loves you to the moon and back and would do anything to see you happy.

Take a moment to write down some of the stories you've been telling yourself. Then I want you to spend some quiet time with your moxie and listen to what it says about those stories. More than likely your moxie is going to call bullshit on them. Be prepared for some hard truths. Be prepared for some discomfort. But by now you know that's the only way you're going to experience growth.

It's time to stop lying to yourself and start listening to your truth.

Wear Your Badges With Pride

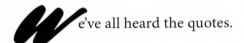e've all heard the quotes.

What doesn't kill you, makes you stronger.

You're only given in this life what you can handle.

If you're like me, and have struggled, you've heard these quotes from people more times than you care to remember. If I can be honest with you, those quotes never helped me to feel any better while I was going through difficult situations. I just think it helped the people who knew me because they really didn't know what else to say.

Part of reclaiming your moxie is understanding and appreciating what you've gone through and had to deal with over the course of your life. As I've said before, we don't know what goes on in the lives of others unless we're told this, so don't assume that just because people are doing well, that they have not struggled or faced adversity. Oh

114

sure, there are plenty of people on this planet who will never know the same struggles as you and me. They have had the privilege of being born into a situation where most everything was taken care of for them during most of their lives. They seem to skate through life without the same care or worry in the world that the rest of us were subjected to. But let me say this, if I'm stuck on a deserted island, playing a game of Survivor, I don't think I want these people on my team. I want people like you and me on my team—those who have gone through a shit-ton of hell in their lives and managed to fight their way back or are in the process of doing so. I want people who have some serious moxie.

It's easy to get caught up in the bullshit and events in your life as it's happening, but if you take a look at the times in your life that have been the most difficult, and I mean really take a look, you start to see just what you're made of. You'll start to feel the power of that moxie. You'll realize that your moxie was always there, even if it was only a slight ember, it was still there helping to guide you along the way. It gave you strength you didn't even know existed. Maybe you're going through something right now. Something so bad that you just want to quit. If so, trust me, that moxie, no matter how diminished, is still there and helping you. Even as a slight ember, it's rooting for you to overcome this challenge. It's waiting for you to get to the point where you can reclaim it and bring it back to that bright shining light it should be.

It is the difficult times in our lives that we are usually the most embarrassed about. The hardships and hurdles we've had to face and overcome. We don't like to talk about the struggles we've been through or the low points we've had, and that is truly unfortunate, because it was during those times that we found our greatest strength and experienced our most significant growth. Although we try to forget them and sweep them under the carpet, we should be looking back at these times with an incredible amount of pride. It was during those times where we earn, what I call, our Badges of Life.

Let's think about this. People play online games where they overcome challenges to collect badges, then proudly post those badges for all to see on social media. *Look at me, I've gotten a "feed my chickens five days in a row" badge. Oh, I've just collected a "beat the wizard" badge. I've "crushed some dumb candy" badge.* I just look at those badges and think, *really*? Is this what we've come to?

So, let's turn this around. Just imagine if people posted their Badges of Life on social media.

I lost my job and my house, but I'm on my way back.

My father was a drug dealer, who stole from his own family, but I am a great parent in spite of him.

My ex was a total asshole who drank his paycheck away and beat me, but I left and I'm doing great.

We grew up without food on the table most nights, but I put myself through college, began a kickass career, and now I mentor kids to help them do the same.

What would happen if we took pride in the challenges we've had to overcome in this life and were truly proud for all that we've accomplished? I think it kind of makes the result much sweeter, don't you? Remember, the badge is not necessarily about the accomplishment at the end; it's in the adversity or challenge you had to overcome to get it. It's in the moxie you had to muster up to move forward, even if you didn't know the outcome.

Many famous people have gotten their Badges of Life by going through some pretty tough adversity. Comedian and game show host, Steve Harvey, was homeless for several years and spent many nights sleeping in his car. Actress Charlize Theron, at the age of 15, witnessed her mother shoot and kill her alcoholic father as an act of self-defense. Oprah Winfrey was molested several times as a child and gave birth at the age of fourteen to a baby who died shortly after birth.

As I've said before, one page does not write your book. Something from your past does not dictate your future. You are stronger than you know. Trust that you are being taken care of and will be victorious as you reach the other side. Believe that what you are going through has a purpose and is going to be used to help someone else get through their adversity. Know that you will be an inspiration to others. We've talked a lot about intention. Set the intention that the reward for all that you have gone through will be great. That you will be blessed with abundance on the other side of this tragedy or struggle.

I know of someone who seemed to have it all; a great job working for a bank, a wonderful family and a beautiful home. When the bubble burst in the housing industry, they were greatly affected by it, and due to certain circumstances, they ended up losing their home through foreclosure. Yeah, that's a tough one. I worked many years as a real estate agent and helped people try to avoid losing their homes. People felt a great amount of shame in facing foreclosure because of the stigma. I used to tell my clients, "No one buys a house with the intention of losing it. Sometimes these things just happen. What's done is done, and now we have to figure out the best way to move on from this with the least amount of damage done to you."

So, whatever happened to the person working at the bank with the great job, family and foreclosed house? Well, their credit took a severe beating, which impacted their ability to be promoted to a higher position in the bank. But I always say that good things happen to good people. When the bank discovered that he had credit issues, they helped him to get out of debt and repaired his credit, so that nothing could stop him from being promoted to that higher position.

See, I always say, that when you do the right thing, you will always be okay. Things that have been lost will be returned. You will always do well. You just need to believe it. Over the years there have been times when I've lost everything I owned. There have been times when I had to start all over in a new apartment with cardboard boxes as furniture and my bed was just a sleeping bag on the floor. I've had to give up pets, belongings, and many other things I never thought I could do without. But guess what? All of the things that I lost were just that—things. They can always be replaced. In fact, they always *were* replaced with more than what I had before.

Our Badges of Life make us who we are. So what badges have I earned during my lifetime? Well, let's see. Not being treated so well by a parent, abusive relationships, bankruptcy, foreclosure, homelessness with four kids, spending some nights sleeping in my car, being on food stamps, and starting all over with nothing to my name. I don't know what other badges might be coming down the road in my future, but as they come, I'll be ready to take them on.

Has it all been bad? No, absolutely not. I spent many years as a research scientist. I got to serve two terms as an elected official, where I did some great things for my community, and I even got my name on a bridge (and no, it's not graffiti). I have had some awesome businesses where I made a lot of money. I've had new cars, boats, a plane, and a vacation home. I have four incredibly beautiful kids who always make me proud. And I know more great stuff is yet to come.

I remember some coworkers once joking with me, saying they wished they had my life. I quickly pointed out that they were only seeing the high points of my life. If they really wanted my life, then they have to have it all, and that included the good and the bad, the highs and the lows. It's a whole package. Everything that has happened in my life has made me who I am today. All the good and all the bad. But where I grew the most was when I faced adversity—when I collected my badges.

What badges have you collected during your lifetime? A crappy childhood? Sexual assault? Divorce? Addiction? Homelessness? Depression? Some other tragedy or adversity? If you can muster up some of that old moxie and see through to the other side, then collect that badge. You've earned it. If you are currently wallowing in self-pity and settling for defeat, do not pass Go or collect $200. The badge sits there waiting for you until you can claim it. Remember to let go of the emotions attached to those badges. You are acknowledging the struggle you've overcome.

I want you to take some time right now and look at those periods in your life where you have struggled and earned those badges. Write them down in your journal. Then write down what you've learned from those periods and how that knowledge has helped you. I'm not only talking about the big things that you've learned during those struggles, but also the smaller things. You didn't collect that badge without learning something and experiencing personal growth. What did you learn about yourself? What did you learn about others? What were you most grateful for?

Ask yourself this, are you going through it, or are you growing through it? Every challenge, every adversity, every badge that you have earned has given you a significant amount of growth. You are an incredible being. Your moxie may have dimmed during those times but know that it continued to flicker to help get you through it. Don't look at those events as a victim. See them as the victor, because that is who you are. Don't be ashamed of your badges, wear them with pride. They've helped to shape who you are and have given you a better understanding of others who have also suffered in this world. I often say that we struggle through things so that we can help others as they struggle.

You've gone through so much. Be proud of all that you have overcome. Wear that badge with pride.

Confidence

When your moxie dimmed so did your confidence. Every failure, every unkind word uttered by another individual, and every limiting belief you've held onto has beat the crap out of your moxie and your confidence. This is a tough one to overcome, but I know you will, because deep down inside you're tired of feeling bad about yourself. You're tired of your limiting beliefs getting the better of you. So, put those beliefs in the past and get ready for some major confidence boosting.

Before we begin, I'm going to ask you to do something incredibly important. I'm going to ask you to start liking yourself. For many of you, this is a herculean task because you've spent so many years of not liking *you*. Liking yourself should be simple, but many of you don't even know how to go about doing it. You focus on the imperfections. You believe the horrible things people have said to you over the years. You've accepted your own limiting beliefs and the limiting beliefs of others. You've told yourself that story over and over again about why you shouldn't be liked.

So, let me tell you right now what a beautiful being you are. You are one of a kind and so special that words cannot even begin to describe it. You were placed on this planet to share your awesome gifts with the rest of us, and although you may not even know what those gifts are yet, trust me, they are there. As you start to reclaim your moxie, and watch your confidence grow, your purpose and the gifts you were meant to share, will come to you. As I said before, everything is temporary. Your confidence is low, but it will rise. You need to start believing in yourself. I know it's hard, but you must. I believe in you. I believe in your ability to do anything your heart desires.

Confidence is important when it comes to moxie, and every step you take outside of your comfort zone, will help you gain back that confidence that so rightly belongs to you. So many times, we get knocked around emotionally, mentally, and spiritually. This takes a toll on our confidence. We start to second-guess ourselves and wonder if we're making the right decision. Sometimes we suffer through such a loss of confidence that we have difficulty making any decisions at all. Should I go left? Should I go right? Screw it. I don't want to make the wrong decision, so I'll just keep going straight down the path that I am already on, or maybe I should just stop.

I'm going to help you regain that confidence by providing you with some exercises. They might seem silly at first, and maybe even outside your comfort zone, but if you're looking for growth, you have to take a step outside that zone.

First, I want you to practice making decisions. Don't worry about whether they're right or wrong. If it makes you feel better, you can practice making decisions about things that don't even really matter. Here are some things you can practice on:

1. Start with a bunch of different colored markers or crayons. Lay them out on a table and then pick one. Don't worry about whether or not it's the right one. Don't over think it. Just do it. Then use it to write down five nice things that happened that day.

2. When you need to get dressed, give yourself ten seconds to decide on something to wear.

3. Ask yourself *Would you Rather?* questions. There are plenty of internet sites that have these questions available for you to answer. Answer them on your own or play with a friend, but don't sit there all day trying to decide on an answer. Answer them quickly.

4. Go for a drive to nowhere. Just let your intuition guide you. Turn when you feel like making turns and try some new roads you've never driven on. Have some fun and explore. There's no planned destination, so there's no way of getting lost. Don't panic. You can always use your GPS to get you back home.

Mirror work is another excellent way of building up your confidence. You might feel really silly doing it at first, but it is necessary that you do it. It's possible that you may not have been told these things throughout your life. You might feel very uncomfortable saying these things to yourself or even hearing these things, but once again, you need to go outside your comfort zone. So, with that said, I'd like you to get in front of a mirror and spend a few minutes just looking at yourself without judgement. Don't worry about the grays in your hair or any wrinkles in your forehead. Just simply look at that person looking back at you. Look into their eyes and know that you have a friend looking right back at you. Take a few minutes and appreciate that beautiful, one-of-kind being in the mirror. Next, I want you to speak to that person in the mirror. I want you to say the following phrases, but begin each phrase by stating your name:

1. I love you.

2. You are a good person.

3. You have so many gifts to share with the world.

4. You are smart and kind.

5. I'm so glad you are alive.

I want you to get your ass in front of that mirror every day and repeat those phrases. You need to say it and to hear it. Because it is the truth. Every fucking word is the truth, and when you say it enough, you will begin to internalize it. Sometimes the only kind thing you will hear about yourself, is what that person in the mirror says to you. You may not think that this simple exercise can boost your confidence and help you reclaim your moxie, but believe me, it can. As your confidence increases, here are some more phrases I'd like you to say, or better yet scream, to that person in the mirror:

1. You fucking rock!

2. You can handle anything that comes your way!

3. There is nothing you can't do!

4. I like you kid. You got moxie!

Once again, I know it seems silly, and you'll probably feel silly at first, but you need to say those things to yourself. Your moxie needs to hear it. Just saying them will raise your vibrational frequency and that is what helps you get a better life.

Here's something else I want you to do. Get yourself out there. The more you network with people, the more you build your confidence and moxie. I know there's a lot of comfort and security in just staying to yourself, but you need to get out and be around other people. We tend to shrink down inside ourselves when we are not feeling confident, but this isolation only does more damage to our self-esteem. Although it's hard taking that first step, rest assured that once you get out there, you are going to feel much better. It's like going to the gym. The worst part is getting off your ass, heading out the door, and making that drive. But once you get there and actually start exercising, you're glad that you made the effort. Look for some groups where you can share your gifts, knowledge, and interests. You need to understand that people are out there and waiting to meet you. They want to talk to you and be friends with you. I call them the people from your planet. They understand you and appreciate you. Get out there and be with them.

I'm going to throw this out there, and don't think I've lost my mind, but if you really want to build confidence skills, consider joining a group like Toastmasters International. They have meetings all over the world so I'm sure there's one near you. Their meetings are all about people coming together and practicing speaking in front of others. Now, for those of you who have just become paralyzed with fright at the thought of speaking in front of people, rest assured, there are many people who went to their first Toastmasters meeting feeling the same way. These meetings are attended by caring, supportive individuals, just like you, who want to build more confidence and help others do the same. Most clubs actually have the feel of a family and they make their meetings lots of fun. There are many different ways to speak in a public setting and members encourage each other as they achieve their own version of success. I even use some of their techniques in my group coaching practice to help build confidence levels in clients. You can visit as a guest for free and see what it's all about. I strongly encourage you to try it. You've got nothing to lose, might actually enjoy it, and could possibly end up with a huge group of new friends. I'm not seeing a downside.

Boost your confidence, boost your moxie. It's as simple as that. Look, you've worked so hard through this book to make some incredible changes in your life. Don't stop here. Believe in the amazingly awesome person that you are. Let that beautiful light shine through. I have always believed in you. Now it's your turn. You've got this.

Surrender

*S*ometimes we just need to let things go. We fight tooth and nail only to become disappointed and frustrated because things didn't go the way we had hoped or planned. We can't get our heads around it; it's beyond our comprehension, and it just seems to cause us a great deal of anguish. I'm going to give you some really good advice here, and that's to let it go. I call it surrender.

Know that you cannot, and it's not even your job, to fix everything.

Surrendering means that you stop fighting certain things and you simply accept them. I'm not talking about being abused or someone mistreating you. This has nothing to do with that. I'm talking about letting go of things you can't control or change in your life. Get into this mindset, especially when it comes to wanting to change people. Stop trying to change others and make them conform to your standards. They are who they are, and unless they decide to change themselves, you're going to have to learn how to accept them the way they are or decide that they no longer should be a part of your life.

Surrender is also trusting that things will work out for you, even if you don't see it, or have any idea how it will happen at that moment. Just know that everything you need will be provided for you. I have found that when I surrender, that is when things usually break loose for me. When I finally stop trying to take control of something and let go of the wheel, that's when I'm steered in the right direction.

I remember hearing Oprah Winfrey talk about an experience that showed how surrender worked for her. Back in her early days, before she was the megastar that she is now, she happened to read a book named *The Color Purple*. This book resonated with her so much that she became obsessed with it. When she learned that there were plans to make the book into a movie, she told anyone who would listen that she planned to be in that movie. She could feel this in her very core and committed to doing whatever it took to make it happen. She ended up going to audition for a part in the movie and read for the role of Sofia Johnson. She noticed that the name of Sofia's husband was Harpo, which was Oprah spelled backwards; another indicator that she should have this coveted part. She knew she was meant for this role. She did everything she could to promote herself and make it known that this role should be hers. Some time went by after the audition and she couldn't believe that she hadn't heard any-thing from casting. She wondered how this could possibly be, so she called the casting director, who let her know straight up that it was *he* who did the calling, not her. He essentially told Oprah that she was a nobody; that they had "real actresses" auditioning for that part. She could not believe what she was hearing and was devastated because she just knew that she was meant to do this. Her self-confidence began to drop and soon she began to think that maybe she didn't get the role because she was "too fat." She went to what she described as a fat farm, where she prayed about the role and tried to understand why she had not gotten it. One day, as she was running around the track, she started praying for help in just letting it go and to make it a point to be happy even if she didn't get the part. She stopped on the track and began to sing the hymn, *I Surrender All*, and as she sang it more, she went from just singing the lyrics to internalizing their meaning. She sang and prayed at that moment to let it all go to a higher power. She accepted that it was out of her hands, and that no matter what the outcome was, she would accept it without bitterness. Just after that moment of acceptance, someone came running out to the track letting her know that Steven Spielberg was on the phone. She got the part. The rest is history.

Know that everything you go through or do has a purpose for you. You may not know what the purpose is at that moment. It may not become clear to you for many years, but trust that there is one. When you get overwhelmed because you can't seem to find that purpose, or think that something should have went your way, but didn't, surrender it. Just let it go and see what happens. When you've done all you can do, surrender.

Surrender is not about rolling over and giving up. It's about doing everything in your power to make something happen and then simply letting it go. Release it. It's like being a candidate the night before an election. You ask yourself, did I do everything in my power during this campaign? Did I leave no stone unturned in my efforts? Did I give it my all? If the answer is yes, then it's time for you to surrender it.

We try to figure out the purpose of things, but we are not always successful. I often joke that I keep looking for the guy in the trench coat—the one that will say, "Psst, come over here. I've got what you're looking for, doll." As I get closer, he will open his coat and show me "the plan." I picture myself nodding as I read what's supposed to happen in my life and say, "Okay, now it all makes sense to me." I haven't seen this guy yet, but if I do, I've got a ton of questions for him.

Sometimes the purpose is vastly different from what we originally thought it would be. When coaching candidates running for political office, we always focused on the end result, which was winning the race, but I often reminded them that winning the election. may not have ever been the purpose for them running—that maybe, there was a different purpose, such as meeting someone or some other event happening along the way, which was the true purpose for them running. I would advise them to run their best race but surrender the end result to their higher power. Often, they would come to me long after the election and let me know that they had indeed encountered something, or someone, along the way that actually set them on a different course.

I want you to stop for a moment and think back to a time where you thought things should have gone a certain way, but they ended up going a different way, and to your surprise, they ended up better than you could have ever thought possible. Was there a time when you thought something was really bad, but it turned out good? Can you think of any instances when you surrendered, and things broke loose?

So, what does surrender have to do with moxie? Surrender is all about having faith that things will go as they should, not necessarily as we think they should. It means that you have done your best to make things happen and then you trust in universal energy or some other higher power that it will happen according to the plan.

It's about letting go of things and acknowledging that we are not in control of everything. Faith, trust, and moxie go hand in hand.

Get Some Faith

*I*n something. In anything.

I don't care what you call it. God, Jehovah, Allah, The Big G, Universal Energy, Spirit—it's all the same. It's something higher and mightier than you, or all of us. In order to gain greater things in this life, on this big blue marble, you'd better start believing that there are other forces at work here. We've become such an arrogant species lately. We seem to think we are totally in control of everything around us and we don't need help from anything greater than us. Many people never think about faith and some people even seem embarrassed to admit they believe in a higher power. They liken it to believing in the Easter Bunny or Santa Claus.

They say that there are no atheists in fox holes, and they may be right, because I know plenty of people who have no faith until something really bad happens, and then all of a sudden, there are some pretty tall order prayers being sent upwards. When all else fails, pray. Pray really hard. But why wait until those perilous moments to ask for help and guidance? Why let things get to such a point in your life where there are very few options left? Shouldn't we be a bit more proactive in the faith department?

I can tell you that allowing faith into your life makes for a much less worrisome life. Think of faith as a magic carpet that glides you above the worries and "hows" in your life. You set the intention, decide where you want to be, and just hop on that magic carpet. You know that everything you need will be provided. You trust in that knowledge. You get in the zone when you align yourself with universal energy and have faith that everything will work out the way you want it to. And once you're in the zone, just watch all the cool stuff that comes your way.

Faith helps to bring about miracles when we didn't think there were any left. Faith keeps you going when most everything else fails. Faith helps you to build trust that there will be opportunities and people put in your path to help you. Whether you call these people angels or not, is totally up to you. Some people call them messengers or spirit guides. Be open to their help and accept it with gratitude. Know that there are no coincidences. The people you meet are put in your life for a reason. I have been blessed with many angels appearing in my life during times of struggle and even when things were going well.

Faith takes over when we can't figure something out or when we can't find a reason for what has occurred. There are some things we cannot explain. We simply have to believe that a power greater than us came in and intervened. When I went through my divorce, the children and I had very little money. I had been a stay-at-home mom and had just gotten my real estate license when we left our home. Most real estate agents work on commission only and there is no such thing as a steady pay check. I had four kids and very little money, so imagine how I cringed when one of them innocently suggested that we should go to McDonald's for dinner. Oh boy, how do I say no to four kids who have just had their lives turned upside down. I remember choking back tears and wondering how I was going to pull off feeding four of them with less than ten dollars in my pocket. As I waited in line, I couldn't help but notice a beautiful woman walk from the side of the restaurant and out the door. I will never forget it. She had long black hair and the most beautiful face I have ever seen. There was something incredible about this woman, although I couldn't exactly say what it was. and I couldn't help but stare at her as she left the restaurant. When it was my turn to order food, I stepped up to the counter and ordered a pathetically small amount of food consisting of an order of chicken nuggets, fries and two sodas to share between all of us. I remember thinking to myself, *it's not enough for them—they're still going to be hungry.* I took the tray of food back to the table and the kids started eating. I remember telling them some story about having a really big lunch earlier that day and that's why I wasn't eating any of the food. One of the kids needed ketchup, so I sent them to the counter to get it. They came back several minutes later, telling me that the guy behind the counter said our other food would be over shortly. When I asked what other food they were talking about, they told me that the man behind the counter said that the pretty lady with long dark hair ordered the food and said to give it to us. When the man from the counter came over with an abundance of food, I asked him about the woman. He told me that she was behind us and described her as the woman that I watched walk out the door before we placed our order. I know for a fact that there was no pretty lady with long dark hair behind us. I watched that woman walk out of the store when we were in line.

How could she have ordered food for us when she was already gone? To this day I truly believe that something intervened for us and the children and I were in the presence of an angel.

There were many angels placed in my path during that difficult time, and other times throughout my life, and there are many angels who are in your path. Believe that they are there and be open to their help. Trust that whatever challenging time you are going though, you will be guided to the other side of it. Know that you will be taken care of. Don't worry about the "hows" of it. Just set your intention and let it go. Surrender it.

Watch and listen for messages to help guide you. Messages come to us through events, people, and our intuition. Be open to the messages. Sorry, but I'm going to harp on that mediation thing again because messages often come through as thoughts, intuition, or simply a "knowing."

Think about some of the angels that have come into your life during the times that you've struggled and thank them in your journal. Take a moment to write some thoughts about your own faith and beliefs. Are they similar to those of your close circle of friends and family? Are you comfortable talking about your faith? If not, why not?

Think about some of the help or guidance you've been given to get through challenging times and set the intention that you will be an angel to someone else who is struggling. Guide someone else to have faith. Faith is a beautiful thing because it takes our worry away. Allow faith to do that for you. Just know that everything will be okay. I have faith that it will.

A Little Kindness Goes a Long Way

I once heard a story about a group of teenage boys who were walking home from school. One of the boys, Rick, noticed another teenage boy standing alone by a tree. He instantly recognized him as the new kid in school and told his friends to go on without him. When they questioned him, he said that he was going to go over to see what the new kid was doing. Of course, his friends gave him some trouble for even bothering with this kid, but he went anyway. Rick introduced himself and they started up a conversation. They walked home together and found they had a lot in common, including a crush on the same girl. They soon became friends and that friendship continued throughout high school. On the day of graduation, the new kid informed Rick, that on the day he stopped to talk to him, he had planned to kill himself. His parents had gone through a bad divorce, they had to move to another town, and he felt isolated. Like many new kids, he was ignored by the established students. He admitted that he was in a place of darkness and thought it would be better if he were not even alive. Rick's simple act of kindness saved a life that day.

Never underestimate the power of a kind word or action. You never know how your words or deeds will affect others. Part of reclaiming your moxie means that you always do the right thing. You show compassion for those who need it. You become an instrument for helping others reclaim their own moxie. Remember, we are here to make a difference in the lives of others. You never know how much of a ripple effect a small act of kindness will make.

I love to tell this story about my grandfather. I credit him for my love of books, which ultimately led to my writing. I can remember as a small child—maybe no more than four years old—visiting him and my grandmother. I would climb upon his lap every week to have him read me a story. My grandfather smoked and he had an ashtray that was on a stand. It was probably around three feet tall. Well, my pile of books stood as high as that ashtray. He would buy me books all the time and just sit there and read them to me. I can remember sitting on his lap mesmerized as he turned each page and read all those books. It is one of the most cherished memories I have of my grandfather.

Many years later I happened to be speaking with my grandmother as she was cooking in the kitchen. The subject of books came up and I mentioned how much I loved my grandfather reading to me when I was young. While still focused on her task, she said so matter-of-factly, "Your grandfather didn't read those books to you."

I thought, obviously, she doesn't remember those days.

"Yes, he did," I said. "He read books to me all the time. Don't you remember?"

"Oh, I remember, but your grandfather didn't read those books. He couldn't read. I guess you don't know that your grandfather never learned how to read."

I sat there for a moment trying to get my head around what she was saying. "Wait a minute, I don't quite understand. How did he read all those books to me?"

My grandmother turned around, looked me in the eye and said, "Your grandfather wanted to do something special for you. He could not read, but he bought the books anyway and made up stories by looking at the pictures on each page. He didn't want anything stopping him from doing something special for his granddaughter."

I looked into the living room and saw my grandfather sitting on the sofa watching one of his favorite wrestling shows. I can't tell you how much my heart swelled at the thought of the beautiful gift he gave me when I was a little girl. Here was a man who could not read, but through his incredible generosity, instilled in me a deep love and appreciation for reading. The lesson of this story is that love and kindness have no boundaries. You have the ability to make a significant impact in someone's life on a daily basis. Don't allow an opportunity to do this go by.

Kindness, and trying to make a difference in the lives of others, is something our society needs more of. We need to spend more time lifting others up instead of tearing them down. We are so quick to judge. So eager to jump on people for mistakes they make. We are quick to speak up yet hesitant to step up. We have no problem voicing our opinion from the safety of a keyboard, but when it comes to acting, we are missing in action. How many times have you seen a video posted of something horrible happening while everyone stands around and simply watches? Everyone has a camera, but no one has a conscience. No one gets involved. No one steps up to help. What does that say about us as a society? It says that we're becoming more detached and less empathetic to others. We have forgotten what it means to be kind and compassionate. If we continue down this road, and don't reverse this trend soon, I'm afraid that our civilization will end with horrific consequences.

But not everyone we come in contact with is kind. So, how do we deal with the jerks and jackasses of this world? We do it by feeling sorry for them. After all, I find it hard to believe that people are born this way. Something happened that made their beautiful light go dim. Their moxie has been cut down to nearly nothing and there is something in their core that makes them lash out at others. As I said before, hurt people, hurt people.

I realize that I'm going out on a limb with this whole kindness and compassion thing for people who aren't so nice. I know our first reaction is to meet their nastiness head on, but I caution you not to get caught up this type of behavior. It's easy to do—a simple tit for tat—and the next thing you know, you're wallowing in the mud with them. You're not changing them, but they certainly are changing you. Do not allow others to change who you are. This is one of the mantras in my household. It can be so easy to sink to the level of others. In fact, it's usually our gut reaction, and we can get caught up very quickly in this trap, but don't allow it to happen. Instead, rise above.

If you encounter someone who is miserable, silently wish them well and be on your way. We all run across these people. They seem to be in a constant state of misery—just a bunch of unhappy curmud-geons. Who knows what's going on in their lives? It's not for us to try to figure out. Our job is to shine our beautiful bright light when-ever and wherever we can. Instead of being sucked into their nega-tive, gloomy energy, try complimenting them about something. Oh, come on, surely you can find something to compliment them on.

That's a nice shirt.

I really like what you did with your hair.

You're really good at your job.

I appreciate you.

It's not about sucking up to people. It's about using your moxie and your energy to affect the people you come in contact with. You don't know what's going on in their lives. You only see the outside. You only see the reaction to something that might be affecting them on the inside. Offering a kind word or phrase can make a person smile and help raise their energy level. It can help them to have a better day compared to how it was before they saw you. Just do it, for cripes sake. Offer up a compliment to someone and watch their reaction. You can actually see a difference in their countenance and mood. After all, don't you feel better after someone has complimented you?

Ok, so now you're asking, what if people are mean to me? I mean, *really* mean to me?

So, here's the deal. Don't confuse kindness with weakness. Being kind does not mean that you have to take crap from mean people. As I said before, we don't always know a person's situation. If it's someone you encounter in passing, just let it go. If it's someone who continuously is not very nice, then you may need to step up and have a serious conversation with them. If you cannot get resolution after trying different methods, then maybe it's time to let them know that their behavior is unacceptable, and you won't tolerate it anymore. Silently wish them well and move on from them. And this includes relatives. You shouldn't take crap from family any more than you should take it from strangers. If you can't get it resolved then it's time to limit their contact with you. Remember, you don't deserve to be treated badly. Besides, you're not going to have time for those type of people. You'll be way too busy seeking out and spending time with other kind people just like you.

Please don't underestimate the power of kindness. Open your heart. Do a good deed. Perform random acts of kindness for others. Not only will the recipient feel good, but so will you. Make your behavior the example that others seek to emulate. Reclaiming your moxie is all about growing that beautiful light inside of you. Kindness is a way to spread that light throughout the world.

Get Out of Your Head

*S*ometimes the only things that hold us back from doing something are our limiting beliefs and our minds. We get so wrapped up in what we think is the truth, that it often clouds our judgement and keeps us from actually doing something that could help us with our personal growth. Often the things we fear, never really happen, and all the worry and anguish were for nothing.

I remember having a blood drive at one of the places I worked. Now, for those of you who give blood on a regular basis, and have never had an issue with it, I commend you. You are superheroes. For those of you who are like me, and break out into a cold sweat at the mere mention of donating blood, you understand where I'm coming from. It's not that I'm squeamish, mind you. I started my career working in the hospital as a med tech drawing blood from others on a daily basis. I have absolutely no problem at all seeing puddles of it on a hospital floor or watching a series like Dexter with splatter stains all over. The trouble comes when it's my *own* blood that I'm seeing. It's kind of like a "being able to dish it out, but not take it" sort of thing.

Going to get my blood drawn for even a routine lab test always provided me with a bit of anxiety. I'd sit in the chair with my mouth suddenly feeling like it was stuffed with cotton and tensing all the muscles in my arm. I may have, although this is not a full-blown admission mind you, but I may have even passed out once or twice.

So, there I was, a member of the employee activities committee, letting everyone in the office know about the onsite blood drive and encouraging them to sign up. I have to admit that I felt a bit ashamed of myself for not signing up, but not ashamed enough to get over my fears. Some of my coworkers secretly admitted to having the same fear of donating blood. I would nod and say, "Yeah, I know what you mean. I'm the same way. I'm not giving blood either."

When the day arrived, I watched as people paraded into the conference room, climbed onto the reclining chairs and chatted with one another. My job was to sit at the canteen station, hand out drinks and snacks, and to keep an eye on people to make sure that nobody passed out. As I sat there handing out little bottles of orange juice, I started to think about my fears and what was actually stopping me from donating a little blood to someone who could really use it. I knew it was all in my head, but that wasn't stopping me from still feeling the fear. The feeling was real. I told myself that if someone who needed a transfusion was sitting right in front of me, I would probably get over my fear to help them out pretty quickly. I kept telling myself. "It's in your head and you need to get over it. The person who needs blood can't be in front of you because they're lying in a hospital somewhere. Just donate the damn blood already."

When fear controls us, and our minds get in the way, we start making up lots of excuses as to why we can't do something, and boy, was this circumstance no exception! Once I told myself that I needed to step up and donate my blood, all the excuses came a-calling. It was if I had those two little people, one on each shoulder, trying to talk me into, and out of, my decision.

"Just donate the blood, you big baby."

Karen, don't you remember that you passed out once when they drew a tube of blood? One crummy little tube? This is a whole bag! What if you pass out?

"No worries, you're in a room with a bunch of professionals who know exactly what to do. There's nothing they haven't seen before. Just let them know you're nervous because it's your first time and you'll be fine."

Karen, suppose you throw up? You could. You could get really queasy and throw up.

"Didn't we just have this conversation about professionals in the room? Besides, there's gingerale right there in the cooler. I'm sure it won't be a big deal if you want to have a sip or two while you're donating blood."

Karen, didn't you just hear someone say that they suggest you drink lots of fluids the night before? The only thing you swizzled last night was a glass of wine. Alcohol dehydrates, you know. Not only didn't you drink lots of fluids, but jeez, now you're actually dehydrated! Dehydrated people always pass out...and throw up.

"For God's sake, just grab a bottle of water from the cooler and drink it. You'll be fine."

Karen, I hate to be a pain in the ass, but the little pamphlet sitting on that chair over there said that you should have a full meal within the last three hours of donating blood. You had nothing more than an apple this morning and a crappy meal of ramen noodles last night. What kind of nutritional value is that? Not only are you dehydrated, but I'd go so far as to say you're sort of malnourished today too. Not only will you pass out, but you won't even have anything in your stomach to throw up. You'll be dry-heaving it in the middle of the floor. Is that how you want your co-workers to see you?

"Ok, you can stop being so dramatic. Look, there's a granola bar sitting right there in front of you. Eat it and relax."

Karen, what if you have to pee right in the middle of the donation?

"Really? Are we really going to go there? Here's something to think about Karen—the blood drive is almost over. You've been going back and forth for the past hour over whether to do it or not. The window of opportunity is closing and then the decision will be made for you. The blood drive will be over, and you will end up regretting it. This is your chance to do something bigger than yourself. It's all in your head. All the fears. All the excuses. Get out of your head and follow your heart. The patient is not in front of you, but you will save one or several lives today."

And with that, a decision was made.

Was I scared when I went to the table and finally registered? You bet I was.

They checked my hemoglobin, which was fine and then they checked my blood pressure. I can tell you that my blood pressure was higher than I had ever seen it because I was so nervous. When I walked over to the donation chair, I made it a point to share my feelings with the attendant who was there to draw the blood. Although I felt kind of silly to admit my fears, I was really proud of myself for sharing my vulnerability with him and asking for help. He was really cool about it and said that what I was feeling was pretty common with first time people. I put in my earphones and listened to some reiki healing music to relax me. The attendant checked on me throughout the whole process, which by the way, only took about ten minutes.

When it was over, I was the one heading over to the canteen table for snacks and drinks. I felt like I was a superhero and told everyone I came across that day about my experience, especially the people who were afraid of giving blood. They thought I was so brave. I told them that it was not one bit about bravery, but all about getting out of my head, because my head was the only thing that stopped me all those years from donating blood. I encourage all you scaredy cats out there, who have been putting off donating blood, to go ahead and do it, because the biggest scaredy cat of them all—me—did it and lived to tell about it.

Maybe you've been telling yourself something all these years that has stopped you from doing something you've really wanted to do or something you know you should be doing. Maybe you've always wanted to start a business, run a marathon, or even take salsa lessons, but you haven't taken those first steps because of that silly little voice inside your head. If you've been allowing your head to stop you from doing something incredibly awesome or scary, then I suggest you put it in its place. Don't allow the fears and excuses to come in and stop you from taking advantage of the opportunities presented to you, because they'll just end up as missed opportunities. Haven't you missed enough opportunities already?

Go for the gold. Reach for the stars. Shoot for the moon. There is nothing stopping you from doing anything your beautiful heart desires except you. The excuses end today. Get out that notebook and start writing down your dreams, your goals, and your visions. Write down what's been stopping you and what you are going to do to overcome it. Chances are that things are not as out of reach as you originally thought. Don't listen to what's being said in your head. Its job is to make you feel safe and comfortable. Its afraid of the unknown and wants to keep you protected from what it deems as failure, but you know that failure is just another name for research. Listen to that moxie deep down inside of you. The moxie that yearns for greatness and knows that you have so much more to give than you've been giving. It's aching for you to break free from your head and follow your heart. Let your moxie be your guide.

See things in a Different Light

love to tell my clients that there are no problems in life, only challenges. I am constantly correcting their sentences because I want them to get into a different mindset—a mindset of looking for ways to overcome challenges. For me, the word problem is negative and final, but the word challenge indicates that it can be overcome. It gets us in the mindset that it is solvable. Change I have a problem to I have a challenge and notice how that feels when you say it. It invites your mind to figure out a solution. Replace the problem is with the challenge is and you won't feel so defeated.

One of my friends, who was trying to do something on a computer, turned to me and said, "I can't do this." I told her "Oh, you can do it, you just haven't figured out a way yet." She cocked her head and looked at me for second. I could almost see the wheels spinning in her mind as she nodded and went back to the challenge at hand. Within a few minutes, she had it figured out. She just needed to change her mindset in order to overcome the challenge she faced at that moment.

Henry Ford once said, "Whether you think you can or think you can't, you're right." Well, Henry's right. We have a lot more responsibility for our outcomes and overcoming challenges than we think. If you think that you can't do something, then you won't. As you know most of the things that stop us exist only in our heads through our limiting beliefs. When we decide to change those beliefs, or alter our mindsets, we experience very different results.

It's like when people tell us to have a good day. In reality, the day will be what we make it. We may not always control the events, but we always control our response to them. Having a good day or a bad day is a choice. Make the choice every day to make it good. Do not allow the hurdles to get to you, drag you down, and stop you from making your day the way you intend it to be. Understand that you are no longer sitting on the sidelines of life. You are in control of more things than you could ever imagine. Accept it. Own it.

Wake up every morning and set the intention of having a good day and not allowing things to ruin it, especially the little things that you tend to get so caught up in. You can start your day with an affirmation to help you set this intention. Affirmations are great tools to help you stay positive. Think of them as custom orders you send out to be filled by the universe. You've most likely been doing affirmations, just not in a positive way. They've been more in the limiting belief category. See if any of the affirmations—um, limiting beliefs— below ring a bell.

I can't lose weight.

I always seem to pick the wrong people.

I'm never going to get out of this dead-end job.

My life sucks.

Like I always say, ask and ye shall be given. Now, since we're talking about seeing things in a different light, how about we try something a little bit more positive. Below are some much better affirmations to begin our day.

Today is a great day.

I am surrounded by love and abundance.

My next job is right on the horizon and it is great.

I attract caring, respectful, and loving people into my life.

Remember, positive attracts positive and negative attracts negative. It's very easy to become negative in this society. We are quick to criticize others and social media only perpetuates this bad habit. Moxie cannot thrive with constant negativity. Now, I'm not asking you to spend one hundred percent of your time with a frozen smile on your face. I am, however, asking you to not get caught up in a negative mindset when things start to become somewhat challenging. I want you to make every effort to get out of the negative mindset that has been keeping you from having and doing great things in life. Stop seeing things as hopeless or problematic. We only have challenges that we haven't yet overcome. Come on, you're no stranger to challenges and adversity. You've been through them. Why is it you've managed to get through the big challenges in life, yet allowed the little ones to stop you in your tracks? The glass is half full. Always.

Your life is worthy of great things. Always. Change your mindset, change your life.

Stop complaining. It's really bad for your moxie because it gets you into a negative mindset. Complaining is insidious and highly contagious. It starts off innocently enough with one tiny little complaint, then the complaints build up to several in a row. Next thing you know, you're complaining to others and walking around looking for other people who also like to complain about things, so that you can have a big old complaint-fest. It starts with one person and quickly spreads to others faster than the plague. I have seen whole departments in organizations take on a negative energy because of people complaining. It draws down your energy and lowers your vibrational frequency. Even if you do not partake in complaining, just having it go on around you, will have the same effect as if you are involved in it.

Complaining is the opposite of gratitude and only ungrateful people complain all the time. How can you expect to get more abundance in your life if you walk around complaining about everything? Think of complaining as a huge energy wall surrounding you. Nothing good can get through it. Abundance gets shut off. I encourage you to get a handle on any negativity or complaining that you have going on in your life. Don't allow yourself to get caught up in it. Challenge yourself to go twenty-one days without complaining. Why twenty-one days? Because experts say that's how long it takes to either make or break a habit.

Complaining puts you in victim mode, and since you are no longer a victim, there's no benefit to complaining. People complain about things because they feel powerless to change them, but that is not you. You have moxie and that gives you power. If you don't like a situation you have the power to change it. You are a fucking super-hero. There's nothing you can't do, so own it.

Reclaiming moxie means that you are going to have to have a major shift in your mindset. You're going to have to think very differently than you've ever thought before. It means that you're going to have to stop complaining and be more positive than you have been in the past. You must not allow people, situations, or events to pull you down. I know this is difficult, but you've been through so much more. You are going to have to listen to that little voice deep down inside you that says keep your head down and just keep pushing through the storm until you can get through it.

I want you to think about how much you complain throughout the day. See if you can remember to record those complaints in your journal. Next, I want you write down what action you need to take to eliminate those complaints. For example, if you're complaining that your job sucks, what action are you going to take to eliminate this complaint? What if you're complaining about not getting respect from your kids? How about when you complain about not having enough money? Don't just complain, take action.

Changing your mindset and your destructive habits can take time. It's easy to get frustrated and fall back into the same old habits, but you've got this. Be gentle on yourself because you may be trying to undo a lifetime's worth of bad habits. If you slip, it's okay—just acknowledge it and get right back on that horse. Seeing things in a different light will provide you with a whole new outlook on life. It will raise your vibrational frequency and open new doors for you. You've come such a long distance in your healing process through-out this book as you reclaim your moxie. Keep it going. You're almost there.

Abundance

Want to get more out of life? Want more wealth, love, or friendship? Then start coming from a place of abundance instead of a place of lack. What you focus on, grows. If you focus on negativity, that is what will grow. If you focus on positivity, that is what will grow.

Don't believe this stuff works? Just ask someone who practices the abundance mindset.

Here's the deal. When you choose to come from a place of lack, and don't believe you are worthy of anything, you get nothing. When you choose to come from a place of abundance, and believe that you deserve great things in life, you receive abundance. It's about setting your intentions and raising your frequency.

Remember what I said earlier about setting intentions and the universe taking your order? Well, that goes for money too. When it comes to the law of attraction, if you want more money, then you need to embrace it and remove all limiting beliefs about money from your mind. Worry and fear over money actually help to keep it away. It stops the flow of money energy, and yes, money has energy. Remember, everything has energy. If you walk around thinking you are poor, and you will never have enough money, then you are right, you won't. Your order will be filled courtesy of the universe. Set the intention of how much money you want to make and remember to be specific. Don't just say, "I want more money," because you might end up finding a quarter on the street and that's it—your request was filled. No matter what you believe, whether you have nothing, or you have abundance, you are correct.

Now, I should make something clear. Abundance is not always about wealth. You are the one who defines your abundance. Some people consider abundance to be enough money to cover their bills and are happy with that. Others consider abundance to be living large as mega millionaires. People can have an abundance of health and love. Abundance for some people is that their needs are always taken care of and they want no more than that. Abundance does not always equal money.

And while we're on the subject of money, I'm going to give you some advice. Get over your limiting beliefs about it. You know the ones that I'm talking about. The ones that make you poor. The ones that will never get you out of debt and into a better, more abundant life. Don't know what I'm talking about? Well, let me remind you of some of those limiting beliefs you may have about money.

I can never make enough money.

Every dime I get paid goes right back out the door.

I never have enough money.

What you focus on, grows. Where has your focus been? Complaining? Negativity? A place of lack? Things that you don't have? Why are you wasting your time focusing on things that have no value to you? If you're going to spend so much time focusing on something, then focus on something that reclaims that moxie. Why not focus on getting a better life? Why not focus on joy, happiness, love, and gratitude. If you want these things in your life, then focus on them. Let's replace those earlier limiting beliefs with the following affirmations.

Money comes to me in many forms.

The opportunities for me to attract more money are endless.

I have abundance and all that I want will be provided to me.

One of the things you can do to help attract more abundance in your life is to create a vision board. A vision board helps you to see things as you want them to be. Don't be fooled by the simplicity, because you would be surprised at the manifestation that can occur from creating them. The vision board supplies consist of poster board which you can get anywhere, magazines that you can get for free from neighbors, some glue, and markers. Once you have all the supplies gathered, take some time to meditate on the vision board. Ask that you be guided to create a board and a life filled with abundance. Next, using the magazines, cut out pictures of things that you want in your life. If you can't find specific things that you want in magazine then print them off your computer. They can be pictures of anything you want—houses, relationships, cars—when it comes to vision boards, the sky's the limit. Glue your pictures onto your vision board along with any words that empower you. Feel free to use the markers to write some empowering words on your vision board. Set the intention that whatever is on that vision board will find its way into your life. Finally, place your vision board somewhere that you can see it every day and envision that whatever is on that board is already yours.

I really want you to take some time to create that vision board, but for now, take a moment to write about abundance in your journal. Picture a life of abundance. What does that mean to you? Does it involve money, good health, satisfying relationships? Is it traveling in a private jet or spending the day in your hammock? Only you can dictate abundance.

Here's the thing about abundance. You cannot simply hope for it. You must see it. You must feel it. You have to understand that it really is already yours. Remember that whole parking spot thing I talked about in an earlier chapter? Well, abundance is the same thing. You see it in your mind. You know it is true. But there's a catch that I should mention, you have to do your part in order for it to happen. You don't just simply say *I'll take a great job and a beautiful house, thank you.* That's not how it works. You must still work hard for it. It's like saying I want to win the lottery, but I'm not going to play. Abundance doesn't come to slackers. Let's say you want a better job. Sitting around talking about it and complaining about your current job is not going to get you to the next level. Set the intention that the better job is in your future then do whatever is in your power to get it. Write a kick-ass resume detailing your great skills, envision yourself in this position, feel what it is like to be in the position, and be positive about the results. Then hop on that magic carpet called faith and allow the universe to do its job to figure out the rest.

Reclaiming your moxie means that you are entitled to the best things that this life has to offer. You are working so hard on becoming whole and figuring out your purpose in this life. You need to start believing, I mean really believing, that abundance is already there for you and all you have to do is set the intention that it will come your way. Remember, abundance is whatever you want it to be. You are not greedy for wanting more things, including money, in your life. These things are already there just waiting for you to claim them. Ask and ye shall be given. Sound familiar? Go ahead and ask.

Find Your Peeps

*Y*ou are known by your peers, and if your peers lack moxie, then so will you.

Who you spend time with is who you become, so who are you spending time with? Are you spending your time with positive people, people who cheer you on and want to see you do well, or do you spend your time with people who are negative, constantly complain, and are bitter about life? Are they just scraping to get by or are they living a life with a mindset of abundance? Do they roll their eyes and say, "Yeah, right" when you talk about your dreams or wanting a better life, or do they give you a big-assed high-five and say, "Fucking right!"?

If you're running around with a bunch of negative Neds or Nancys, then it would be best to part ways. You can't continue to listen to negative people and stay in a positive place, let alone maintain a mindset of abundance and gratitude. Negative people are like energy vampires. They can easily drain you and dim your moxie. Be warned, they will try to pull you down to their level because, let's face it, misery loves company and complainers love to pull people into their complaint circles. I'll admit it's pretty easy to get drawn in to this type of behavior, but complaining only keeps negativity around you, and it puts you in victim mode. Remember, you are not a victim. Moxie does not accept victims.

As you begin to raise your standards, experience incredible growth, and reclaim your moxie, you will find that there are people in your life who will be uncomfortable with the new you. They liked you the way you were because you were familiar. You had so much in common with them such as low vibrational frequencies, limiting beliefs, and a negative mindset. But as you started reclaiming your moxie, your frequency raised and theirs didn't. Trust me, both you and they will notice the difference. Although it will be uncomfortable, I implore you not to sink back down to their frequency level in an effort to go back to being one of them. Here's the hard truth—you are not one of them. The sooner you break free from that circle the better off you will be.

I know this is going to be a tough thing to ask of you, but I'm going to do it anyway. Delete the need to be liked. Oh, I just felt some readers cringe at this suggestion. After all, who doesn't want to be liked? I get it. It's great to be liked, but are you being liked by the right people? We spend a good portion of our lives wanting the wrong people to like and accept us. Sometimes we outgrow those around us who no longer have the same standards or values that we have. It just happens. Trust me, you're not doing yourself any favors by staying in those circles.

Remember, you are reclaiming your moxie and you don't need nay-sayers holding you back. And this includes family. I know—they're family—but if they're constantly sucking the life out of you, it's going to start having an effect. If you don't want to banish them from your life, then I strongly suggest that you start limiting your time with them. You may want to take them in smaller doses to protect yourself from their energy. Look, I get it, we all dream of an ideal relationship with family members, but sometimes you just have to come to the realization that it's just not possible. I know it's hard to accept, but the sooner you accept it, the better off you will be.

Start surrounding yourself with people who are just like you, who have the same desires and values as you, and who are continually seeking self-improvement. I call them the people from your planet. Others call them their tribe. Whatever you call them, you will recognize them immediately because they are just like you. They have the same mindset as you and operate at the same vibrational frequency. I get so excited when I meet someone from my planet. We greet each other like we're long lost friends. There is a certain energy that gets generated when we're together. My best friend, Adrienne, is from my planet and when I talk to her about meeting other people from our planet, I don't even have to describe them. She knows who I mean, because they are just like us.

Make the effort to find your people. Seek them out. Trust me, you will know them when you meet them. You will instantly click. We already talked about you getting yourself out there and networking. This is a great way to find your peeps. There are plenty of groups, both social and professional that you can find online, to meet up with people who have the same interests and energy as you. As you continue to reclaim your moxie you will attract those who are more like you and want to see you succeed in whatever you set out to do.

Just think, there are people just like you, out there who are trying to find you, because they're searching for their peeps too.

Grab your journal and describe the people from your planet. What kind of people are they? What do they like? What are their personality traits? Write down their description as best as you can because you are putting in that order with the universe.

Reclaiming your moxie means that you're going to have to take a serious inventory of who is currently in your life and who is worthy of staying in your life. And I mean worthy. You are no longer going to allow people in your life who are not worthy of you. Reclaiming your moxie means that you will no longer settle for less than you deserve. You are an incredible human being, who has so much to give to this world. Spend your time with the people who encourage and support you, who recognize your value, and who want great things for you. I realize that the time in between saying goodbye to people who are no longer good for you, and saying hello to your new peeps, could result in a period where you are alone for a bit. I know some of you may be scared by that thought, but don't be. It's just a small transitional phase. There is usually a lull, before a period of growth. Trust me, it will not last forever. Take that time to reflect on all the work you've done to reclaim that moxie. Use it to set the intention that you will be surrounded by lots of your peeps. I love being surrounded by my peeps. In fact, I think many of them are probably reading this book.

Commit to Be Fit

We've spent most of this book dealing with the mental, emotional, and spiritual aspects of reclaiming your moxie. But I would be doing a big disservice to you, my friend, if I did not deal with the physical aspects of it. Remember, as a coach, my job is to help make you whole and that includes mind, body, and spirit. Moxie thrives when everything is in balance and that includes your physical form. We live in a society where obesity has become a serious epidemic and health related issues, such as diabetes, high blood pressure, heart disease, and cancer continue to increase due to our poor lifestyle choices.

Now, before I go on about the physical aspect, I want to make something incredibly clear. I am not asking you to become a body builder, or knock your weight down to something a supermodel would be proud of, unless of course that is what you desire for your physical being, in which case, I say go for it. I am simply asking you to consider where you are now, when it comes to your physical health, and decide where you want to be. It's possible that you are absolutely fine with your physical form and feel no need for improvement, and if that's the case, many kudos to you, but if you're like most of us, then you need to think about making some changes.

What kind of changes you ask? Well, that answer is entirely up to you. If you were looking for me to dictate your diet, or put you on some sort of rigorous physical regiment, I'm sorry to disappoint you. Just like meditation, there is no one-size-fits-all when it comes to making improvements to your physical health. You will have to decide what works best for you. Do your research. Talk to your physician.

I find, that as you begin to reclaim your moxie, there is a natural progression for people to want to make changes or improvements to their physical health. It makes a great deal of sense if you think about it. When you start to feel better mentally, emotionally, and spiritually you automatically want to feel better physically. You've had lots of changes going on so far, so be prepared for a few more.

What kind of changes would you like to make? Losing some of that extra weight you've been carrying around? Getting your glucose or cholesterol levels down to a manageable level? Quitting smoking? Maybe you just want to start eating a bit healthier. It's your physical form, and you're the one who controls it. The important thing is to figure out what you would like to do, set your intention, and then get started.

Effective and long-lasting change is created in small shifts. When you are looking to make changes, especially when it comes to your health, don't start going crazy all at once because it's just not going to work. It's like when you wake up on New Year's Day with that big resolution to lose weight and get back into shape. So, you join the gym, or you go on some restrictive diet where you're only allowed to eat grass clippings and a teaspoon of peanut butter each day. You go gangbusters for about two weeks, maybe three if you really have some stamina, and then fizzle out by the end of the month. You say screw it, give up, and you're right back to the same old routine. You end up accomplishing nothing except for beating the crap out of your morale.

So, instead of going crazy, how about you start with something small? Instead of trying to do ten miles on the treadmill, maybe you can start by just taking a walk every day. Start with a small distance and work your way up. If you don't like to walk alone, then see if you can enlist a friend to walk with you to keep you company, or if you're feeling really feisty, you can start a walking group at work or in your neighborhood. Instead of going on some restrictive diet where you constantly complain about being hungry or giving up everything you like to eat, maybe you could start small by eating less sugary foods in between meals or eating more fruits and vegetables. You could try eating smaller portions. You could commit to drinking more water. Think about taking some fitness or yoga classes. And let's not forget meditation. It's good for the body and the mind. If you can master one or two of these small things, then you can start to add others into your routine. Baby steps. Remember what I said earlier in the book about waking up on the morning of the Boston Marathon and deciding to run? Well, the same goes for getting healthier. I have found that if I make small changes in my routine for my health, I am much more likely to stick with them. Staying committed to a new routine can be a challenge, so you might want to think about making a chart to keep track of things, getting an accountability partner, or even hire a coach to keep your ass in line. I have found that when you spend money on coaching, you tend to commit more to the process.

You can drive yourself absolutely crazy trying to keep up with every fad diet to hit the market in an effort to lose weight. Low carbs, no carbs, no meat, lots of meat—many of these diets work in the beginning, probably because you're throwing your metabolism off by making drastic changes, but it's often difficult to stay on them. Many people plateau or get frustrated because they don't like the food they are forced to eat. They run into problems because they take things to an extreme, or take big steps, instead of making small shifts. Shift your focus off of the weight and onto being healthy. The weight loss tends to follow.

Does getting fit mean that you can't ever have a candy bar, beer, or some other little indulgence for the rest of your life? The answer is no. You might want to re-read the chapter on Self-Care as a reminder to treat yourself to something special once in a while without feeling guilty. When you hit some milestones in your effort to become healthier give yourself a reward. Feel good about your health accomplishments and celebrate them. As you continue the process of reclaiming your moxie you should be celebrating lots of things. Look, I like a big glass of wine and a greasy pizza as much as the next person, but I just commit to not having them every day.

I want to take a moment to give you a preemptive kick in the ass for when you "fall off the health wagon." Not for falling off the wagon, mind you, but for the act of beating yourself up when you do. Call me psychic, because I already know how this is going to go. You start out with lots of good intentions—you've lost some weight, started eating better, or you've really cut down on your smoking—things are going great. Then something happens. Something stressful. The shit hits the fan, and you end up making a choice that is not conducive with your new healthier lifestyle. You fall off the wagon, and here is where you start making that selfdestructive, guilty, downward spiral.

You start beating yourself up and feeling bad because you allowed something to get the better of you. This is where you say to yourself, without even realizing it, "Fuck it, I can't do this." Well, I'm here to tell you that you *can* do it. Remember, one page does not write your book. The wagon is still right there. It hasn't gone anywhere. It's simply waiting for you to climb back up on it and continue on your journey. Let me remind you of the definition of moxie. Tenacity. Grit. Determination. No one's path to a better health is ever done without many challenges. Some of the challenges are not so bad, while some of them seem almost impossible. As things fall into place, and you begin to feel better, you will make better choices when it comes to taking care of your health.

You've got this, my friend.

Use the Good China

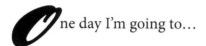ne day I'm going to...

Someday I plan on...

Fill in the blanks and you'll be staring at your goals, dreams, and desires. We set up this imaginary and arbitrary timeline for ourselves. We commit to doing something without actually committing. It's safe. It means we don't have to do it right now. It means we don't have to take a chance and put it all on the line at this very moment. We can talk about taking action without really taking it. We've found a loophole for future success, even if it only exists in our minds.

One day. Someday.

How many people have gone to their graves with a goal of one day or someday, but never actually saw those days come to fruition? How many people have put off their goals, their dreams, and their desires because they're afraid to take a chance or that they might fail? Their desire for safety and feeling secure, along with their fear, stopped them from living their lives on their term as they always wanted.

What are you waiting for?

Think about it like this—what if you only had five more years to live on this planet? Would you have the same job? The same relationship? The same circle of friends? Would you be doing the same things with your life? What would change? Take a deep look inside and ask yourself what is stopping you from doing what you've always wanted to do? What is holding you back? Are you waiting for things to get better? Circumstances to be more perfect? More time? More money? We can't predict the future. These things may never happen, and if you're waiting on these things to occur before you finally do what you've always wanted, you may be waiting for the rest of your life without ever doing them.

Don't let one day and someday hold you back, or stop you, from doing what you've always dreamed of doing. It may never be the right time. Things may never be perfect enough. One day and someday are barriers. They serve no purpose other than to hold you back from achieving your goals and enjoying life. They are the things we say to put off doing what we dream of because we're afraid to fail or even take a chance. I know it sounds strange, but sometimes we even put things off because we're afraid of the success that might come along. Why would you be afraid of success, you ask? Because it can feel foreign to many people. They think they will be held to a higher standard, one they might not be comfortable at. Sadly, many people don't feel as though they deserve success, so they put off finishing things as a form of self-sabotage. If it's not complete, then there can be no judgement, or failure, or even success.

I used to say that one day/someday I'll write a book. I said that for almost twenty years. It was so easy to push off. I had no problem saying it, I just had a problem starting and committing to it. Once I sat my ass down and committed to the process, I found that twenty years worth of thoughts came pouring out of me. Writing the book was easier than I thought it would be. I distributed it to some friends and colleagues for simple edits and felt really good about the process and the book. As I started doing more rewrites and thinking about getting the book to the publisher, I can tell you that I started to feel sick to my stomach. Suddenly, all the gremlins started rearing their ugly heads. Who was I to write a self-help book? What could I possibly have to say that people will want to read? People who write self-help books have it all together—I lose my shit on a daily basis. Who's going to listen to me? It was so weird. I didn't feel this way in the beginning of the book-writing process. In fact, I was super confident that this book would help many people, but that was because I was still in that one day/someday mindset. The closer I got to finishing up this book the more I started to question myself. The process of full commitment, and the fear of being judged by others, made me want to grab all those pages of paper and run to the nearest trash bin. I think I even hyperventilated once or twice. So, here's the deal—when something seems scary it's because it's out of our comfort zone. It's because it's unfamiliar to us, but that's when we start to experience the most growth. Don't be afraid to grow. Take that step.

People put off many things waiting for that perfect time. In the meantime, time ticks away and before you know it, it's too late. They end up with nothing left but regret for not doing what they said they would one day, or someday, do. No one ever went to their deathbed wishing they had spent more time at that suck-ass job or being with that person who was never right for them from the beginning. They go to their deathbeds wishing they had not been so afraid to take that step and do the things they always dreamed of. Don't go to your deathbed wishing you had done more in this life. This is not a dress rehearsal. You only get one chance. Just do it.

Let's use the good china as an example. You know what I'm talking about. It sits there on shelf, proudly displayed without ever being used. Perfect and pristine, but without enjoyment. The owner waits for the right meal to break out the good china, but all too often, the right meal never occurs, and so the china just sits. There's never a meal good enough or special enough for this china. One day it will get used. Someday it will get used. But those days never come. So, let me tell you what really happens to that china. The owner dies and it gets passed down to the next generation who, isn't as fond of it, or doesn't appreciate it as much as the previous owner, so it either gets used, donated, or sold at a yard sale. And all that time the original owner could have enjoyed it, but they didn't because they were too busy waiting for one day or someday.

One day is today. Someday is today.

The time to do things is now. Think about what you want to do. Is there a business that you've always wanted or dreamed of starting? Is there someplace you've always dreamed of traveling to? Is there a job or career you've thought about changing? Where do you live? Are you happy there, or is there someplace else you'd rather be? Who do you want to be with? Are you with the right person? Are they good for you? Do they bring out the best in you or the worst?

I know that change is hard, and sometimes downright scary. The thought of it will many times stop us in our tracks. It comes with a lot of anxiety, self-doubt, and second-guessing, but it can also come with great rewards. Change, especially substantial change, forces us to grow in a way we never thought we could.

Take that chance. Take that risk. Do you itch to quit your job and sail around the world? Do you want to climb the corporate ladder and become president of the company? Do you want to say goodbye to the rat race and write that awesome book you've talked about all these years? What are you putting off? What's on hold? What is life like right now for you? What do you want it to be? If there is a major gap between those two last questions, then set a plan in motion to do something about it. You have total control. Use it. You will continue to do what you've always done until you make the decision to change it. Seems to me like you've got a choice to make. Are you going to go big or go home? Are you going to keep playing small or are you going to step up to something great? Are you going to take advantage of every opportunity that this life has to offer you or are you going to go to your grave regretting your choice to do nothing?

Change your mindset. Turn your shoulds into musts. Stop saying "I should do this" and replace it with "I must do this." Begin to get clear on your intentions and then set them. What do you truly want in life? Where do you want to be? Who do you want to be with?

Listen to that voice deep down inside you. What does it say? Don't tell yourself that your dreams are too lofty, or your goals are too high. I'm here to tell you to go ahead and dream big. Go for the gold. You have my full permission to go as big or as high as you want. Don't worry about what anyone thinks. Don't worry about what anyone says. Who cares? Are you going to listen to your detractors, or are you going to listen to the only person in this world who matters? That's you, you big awesome fireball of moxie! I often wonder why we spend so much time asking others what they think when we have the answers right inside us. My clients *always* have the answers inside them. My job is to condition them to hear that voice. It guides you and won't ever let you down. You are the voice. Listen to your voice.

Let me make this very clear. We are not guaranteed another minute on this planet. Stop waiting for the right moment. Take that step.

Be bold.

Use the good china.

Share the Moxie

*R*eclaiming your moxie is a beautiful thing, but you need to know that a full tank of moxie comes with a lot of responsibility. You can't just reclaim your moxie and simply walk away. No, my love, it doesn't work that way. You have a duty to share it with others and the world around you. You need to understand that you are here for a reason. You have a purpose on this planet, and you must fulfill it. Don't know what your purpose is yet? That's okay. It will become clear. My advice is to meditate on it and be open to the answer and the clues that come your way.

Moxie knows love. It embraces love. Total over-the-moon unconditional love. Trust in that love and be guided by it. You have a covenant with universal energy, with the people and creatures on this planet, and with the planet itself, so be a symbol of hope. Having moxie means that you will be a warrior for injustice and an agent for change. You will be courageous in your beliefs. It is your absolute duty to shut down hate because hate dims that moxie flame in all of us. It is also your duty to speak up for those who do not have a voice. Remember, it was not that long ago that you did not have yours.

Reclaiming your moxie means that you lead by example. From now on you lead, not follow. You become the person that others want to emulate. You watch your words as they are spoken so that they are not unkind. You use your words to uplift and inspire others instead of tear them down. You use your strength and passion for good. You encourage others to believe in themselves and in their dreams because they may struggle to do it on their own. You will become a beacon of light because there are so many people out there who struggle in the darkness and need guidance to help them reclaim their own moxie.

When you reclaim your moxie and show gratitude for all that you have, and all that you will be given, abundance will follow. It is imperative that you show an infinite appreciation for this abundance. Be grateful for not just the big things in this life, but also the small. Especially the small things, because those are the things that tend to be the most forgotten. The act of gratitude needs to be all-encompassing so that you fully understand this beautiful gift which has been given to you. The gift of moxie.

Moxie means that you step up. Know that mediocrity is no longer acceptable—you'll cringe at the very thought of it. You have an intense fire burning inside of you. When your moxie is running at full throttle, you are destined for greatness. It's time to abandon the fear that you've had all those years. It's time to take leaps of the heart as you pursue your dreams. Seek out that which gives you joy and don't worry about what others think. Let them be guided by their own moxie. You are guided by yours.

You have the opportunity to make a difference. You have the ability to make an impact on this world. The moxie that you are reclaiming is so big and fiery that there is no way you can keep it contained. It yearns to burst through your physical being to touch everyone you meet. So, share it. Share that big beautiful ball of light and know that, in doing so, you are helping to heal the world.

The Beginning

While most books call the last chapter The End, I am calling mine The Beginning. That's for two reasons. First, it's my book and I can call the chapters any damn thing I want, but second, and more importantly, this really is the beginning—the beginning of a whole new life for you. I am so excited for you because I know that you are going to do some incredible things in this life, and you deserve it. You have been through some difficult times. You have had your moxie trampled on and dimmed, but as I said before, it was always there—even if it was just an ember. It never left you.

Reclaiming your moxie is not something that happens overnight. It took you a while to lose it, so be gentle on yourself if it takes you a while to get it back. But the good news is that you've already started to get it back. It's all about taking one step at a time as you grow and heal. I want you to know what an amazing being you are. You are smart, courageous, and beautiful. You have so much to offer this world and I can't wait to see you get started. Know that I will be with you, cheering you on every step of the way.

Your journey has been just that—your journey. It is custom made just for you by you. Only you can decide which paths to take. If you don't like one path, or it doesn't seem to be going in the direction you originally thought it would—no big deal—then just move to another one. Remember, there is no such thing as failure, only research. In every result you didn't expect, you learned something from it and that's a good thing. Be grateful for all that you've learned along the way.

I am so grateful for the opportunity to serve you through my own life experiences and for the connection we have made through this book. We are all connected on this planet and that is why it's so important to be there for each other. The process of writing this book was also a way for my moxie to continue to grow. Remember, you are loved by this universe, and all that you need and desire is right there for you. Just set your intention and ask for it. Show gratitude for all that you have and be compassionate for those who still have a long way to go.

You were given that moxie for a reason. You have a purpose to fulfill in this life. Share your gifts, don't keep them a secret. We're all waiting to see what they are. Use that voice—you know the one you were keeping quiet all those years. Stand tall. Be proud. You are going to kick some ass in this world. Stay in touch and let me know how you are doing. I want to read about your challenges, accomplishments, and successes. I can't wait to meet you in my travels and hear about the incredible changes you've made in your life. And don't be surprised if you hear me say those beautiful words...

I like you kid, you got moxie.

Resources

I've created a list of people and things I refer to throughout the book. By no means is this list as extensive as it should be. It's just the basics to get you started. Your journey will guide you to many more books, workshops, and speakers as you increase your knowledge and reclaim your moxie. My intention is to provide you with a more extensive list on my website. Please visit me at www.karenwahner.com

Meditation Apps

Headspace

Insight Timer

Both of these apps have a multitude of different meditations for you to try out, included guided and unguided. Remember, one size does not fit all. Explore each one or look for another app that helps you with your meditation practice.

Mindfulness

palousemindfulness.com

This is a FREE 8-week course to help you with mindfulness. Everything you need is here, and if you finish, you get a cool certificate. Consider this a gift from the heart courtesy of Dave Potter.

Law of Attraction

The Secret by Rhonda Byrne (Book and Movie)

Metaphysics

A Course in Miracles published by the Foundation for Inner Peace (Book, App, and website- acim.org)

University of Metaphysics (Online education for people studying metaphysics) universityofmetaphysics.com

Energy Healing

Healingtouchprogram.com

Reiki.org

Therapeutictouch.org

As promised, here are some books by my favorite authors and speakers. This list is not extensive so be sure and check out other books they've written.

Will Bowen

A Complain Free World: How to Stop Complaining and Start Enjoying the Life You Always Wanted

Jen Sincero

You are a Badass: How to Stop Doubting Your Greatness and Start Living an Awesome Life

You are a Badass at Making Money: Master the Mindset of Wealth

Tama Kieves

This Time I Dance! Creating the Work You Love

Inspired & Unstoppable: Wildly Succeeding in Your Life's Work

Tony Robbins

Awaken The Giant Within: How to Take Immediate Control of Your Mental, Emotional, Physical, and Financial Destiny!